What I love about these essays is how they capture a very particular but strangely ineffable way of being in the world. They tell stories of smart people doing battle with the stupidities that surround them, of adulthood thwarted and childhood cheated and the heartbreaking ways that our dreams both sustain us and bury us. Throughout it all Joe Oestreich is wise, good humored, and deeply literary. I read *Partisans* in fits of recognition and admiration. It's a formidable collection by a genuine talent.
—**Meghan Daum**

Joe Oestreich is the begotten son of Mitchell, Didion, and McPhee—but also an absolute original. These essays cover so much ground and break new ground at every step. Playful, rebellious, searching, Oestreich takes us through disparate landscapes while making of each one a place and people we come to know intimately. And what we discover is not our differences but our glaring commonalities. *Partisans* is the best essay collection I've read in years, from a writer working at the highest level of the craft.
—**Brad Land**

In these punchy, often very funny personal essays, we get snapshots from a well-considered life both home and abroad, at childhood and beneath the shadow of middle age, in the barber's chair and onstage at your local rock club. Joe Oestreich writes with such a warm voice and an easy closeness, I spent most of these pages feeling as if he were across a bar table from me and we were making a rowdy evening out of his gifts for storytelling.
—**Elena Passarello**

PARTISANS

Essays

Joe Oestreich

Black
Lawrence
Press

Black
Lawrence
Press

www.blacklawrence.com

Executive Editor: Diane Goettel
Book and cover design: Amy Freels

Published 2017 by Black Lawrence Press.
Printed in the United States.

For my mom and dad.

Contents

I. HOME & AWAY

The Mercy Kill

1985. I was fifteen and staring hard down the long barrel of summer. My dad had just left my mom for another woman, and this hit me like a bag of bricks. It was proof positive that I didn't know, couldn't know, anyone. Not really. Not on the inside, past whatever veneer they'd doctored up and spit-shined. Easier to stick to the few things I could count on. The ball, the bounce, the basket. Every night after dinner I'd shoot free throws in the driveway. Toeing the mark on the blacktop that served as the foul line, I'd flip the ball to the ground three times and take aim at the hoop my dad had once paid some guy to attach to the garage roof.

My mom would come out the front door trailing Rex—a dog we'd owned for at least ten years, since the days when my parents' marriage was solid, and who, despite the name, was female. "Joe, doll," she'd say, "please remember to open the garage when you play ball." She'd thumb toward a cracked window on the garage door, one of several I'd broken shooting baskets that summer. "I'll have to ask John Parsons to fix that." John Parsons lived five doors down, and my mom walked with him and his dogs religiously, every night as soon as the dishes were done. She had since March, when my dad moved out.

Dribbling the ball, I'd watch her follow Rex down our elm-lined street. We lived in Worthington, Ohio, home of the middle-class dream exemplar. She'd walk past houses that were all variations on an aluminum-sided theme. She'd pass lawn sprinklers firing tracers across grass so green it looked straight off the sod farm. She'd pass the open maws of two-car garages: American sedan for him, foreign hatchback for her, hand-me-down beater curbed out front for the kid. My mom was an adjunct at Columbus Technical Institute, and on the side she taught English to Vietnamese refugees, so she was too busy grading papers and running my sister Jill to soccer practice to maintain our home at the Worthington standard. Our aluminum siding was moldy. Our lawn was pocked with brown patches and turd piles. Our garage door was blackened with basketball dimples, and every time I opened it like my mom asked, I'd see a Pennzoil stain where my dad's '77 Grand Prix should have been.

My dad was never much of a honey-doer, so our place had always looked sort of neglected. Now it was worse. Recently, though, John Parsons had offered to help my mom around the house. "Anything you need, Mary Anne," he'd told her. "Yard work. A broken dishwasher. Car trouble. You call me." And when the battery in her VW Rabbit died, she called him. When the garage door went off the rails, she called him.

John was my friend Steve's stepdad. Steve's mom, friendly in a neighborly way, didn't mind lending her husband out for the odd house repair and seemed happy enough that he had a dog-walking companion. An ex-high school chemistry teacher, John had left the classroom to go out on his own as a handyman. A few times already that summer, Steve and I had squeezed into John's cigarette-smelling El Camino, and he'd taken us along to a job site. Paid us a few bucks to help him paint a room or trim a row of bushes. As we drove home to prim-and-proper Worthington, with John's tools rattling in their buckets and wall primer streaking my mall-bought Levi's, I was both proud and embarrassed. Proud, as a kid who now lived with his mom and sister, to be led by John into the hands-on, get-'er-done world of men. And embarrassed to be seen with a man so unlike my dad—PhD, licensed professional counselor, director of a rehabilitation facility for the disabled—a white-collar guy who paid grunts like John to do jobs like hang basketball hoops.

As my mom and Rex walked up John's driveway, he and his two fat beagle-mixes would be waiting on the porch. From there they'd head down to the ball fields at the elementary. Standing in the grass, watching the dogs run, John would mostly talk and my mom would mostly listen. He was stocky and bolt-strong, smart and well read. Knew something about everything. She was not quite five feet tall, an Adult Education PhD who loved opera and Agatha Christie. Maybe my mom liked John precisely because he was so different from my dad. Maybe she just liked the company. Or the ritual: Walk after dinner, because that was the routine, like Mass every Sunday morning and *Masterpiece Theater* every Sunday night. These were the things she could count on.

When she'd come home an hour or more later, I'd still be shooting baskets, though it was too dark to see the rim. "Oh, boy," she'd say, smiling as she let Rex loose in the front yard. "Didn't we have fun?"

I'd drop the ball in the corner of the garage by the rake and the shovel, neither of which had been used in a long, long time. I'd shut the garage door, which, thanks to John, now went up and down ten times smoother than my jump shot. And I'd follow my mom and Rex inside, a little bit happy because she seemed so happy, and a little bit grateful because John had reached out to her, to us.

What I didn't know, couldn't know, was that my mom and John Parsons would walk the dogs together nearly every night for three years. And they'd keep doing it even after John was charged with murder.

***

Playing ball in the driveway that summer, looking up and down the street at the aerated perfection of the other lawns, at the white-washed siding on the other houses, I wondered if the families living in those homes were as flawless and faultless as was their landscaping. I worried that we were the resident freaks on the block, not just because our house was below par but because we were guarding a secret history, one that I knew to keep hidden from the neighbors.

The secret was that my mom had been a nun and my dad had been a priest. They met in the late sixties in Madison, Wisconsin, where my dad was pastoring a parish and they both were attending grad school. After leaving their orders and quitting their dioceses, they were married in a city hall ceremony across the Illinois state line. Their families were shocked, my dad's especially, embarrassed by the stories in the Madison newspaper that reported he was stepping down from his post with the church. His parents wouldn't talk to him, his sisters wouldn't visit, and my mom and dad spent their first Thanksgiving and Christmas together, alone. By the time my sister and I were teenagers, the scandal within the family was long over, but still we understood that we weren't to discuss our parents' pasts outside the house. Not because they were ashamed, my mom told us, but because they'd never be able to meet other peoples' expectations for how a nun and priest should live. Impossible, she said. Best to keep it quiet. So we did. And as far as my sister and I knew, nobody knew. Except for maybe John Parsons. It was the kind of thing he and my mom would have talked about on their walks.

One night that summer, John's wife knocked on our front door. From up in my room, I could hear that she was crying. Something about John getting so mad he'd ripped the staircase banister right off the wall. My mom slipped into nun-counselor mode, calmly consoling John's wife, then making a bed for her on the couch. As I went back to sleep, I took a strange comfort in the Parsons family's troubles, because it made my family seem a little less screwed up.

The next evening, my mom and John walked the dogs like always, and I never once thought that she probably shouldn't be spending so much time with a guy who could send his wife crying to the neighbors in the middle of the night. I was glad my mom had a man in her life, even if that man was married, even if he could get pissed-off enough to yank down a staircase railing. I wasn't even a little worried that John might hurt my mom. He'd never so much as raised his voice to her. He was polite and deferential as a deacon.

***

As summer unwound, I played Wiffle Ball and badminton in John's backyard. Slapped together bologna sandwiches in his kitchen. Spent a few nights sleeping over with Steve. John would stay up late with us, watching *Scarface* or *The Terminator*, shoot-'em-up movies I wasn't allowed to watch at home. To get us through the boring parts, he'd thrill us with stories of real-life blood and gore, tales from his tours in Vietnam. One night he told the story of how he'd assassinated a Viet Cong general. From five-hundred yards. A single shot.

"Holy crap," I said.

"It was no big deal," he said. "They had me doing that kind of stuff all the time."

What a badass, I thought. Pacino and Schwarzenegger had nothing on John Parsons. I asked if he'd won a bunch of medals. I asked if I could see them.

He brushed that idea away with a wave of his calloused hand, saying that the missions he'd carried out were so covert, the government had expunged his service record in the name of national security. "Medals are for rank and file," he said. "Special Forces don't need no stinkin' medals." Then he smiled. "You want to see something really cool?"

I was fifteen. Of course I did.

"Then hang on. I'll be right back." Leaving Steve and me on the couch with Cokes sweating on the coffee table and Fritos bags bunched between our legs, he headed out to the garage. When he came back, he was carrying a gun that looked like the one from *Rambo*. "This is my baby," he said. "The UZI."

The gun was sinister as a rattlesnake. "Can I touch it?" I said, not quite sure I wanted to.

"You can do better than that," he said, and he extended the UZI toward me. "You can hold it. You can aim it."

I'd never before held a gun, not even a BB. My parents were pacifists. They'd taken me to Vietnam War protests when I was still in the stroller. Back when my dad was a priest, he'd led the Dane County chapter of Clergy and Laymen Concerned About Vietnam, riding around town with a peace-sign sticker on his motorcycle helmet. Not only had I not been allowed to own toy guns, my mom had a conniption every time she caught me extending my thumb and pointer finger, taking aim at my sister. If she knew John was letting me near a real machine gun, she would have strung him up and field-dressed him, pacifist or not.

"Don't worry," John said. "It's not loaded." He pushed the UZI into my chest. "Here. Take it."

I was expecting cold steel. I was expecting the gun to have a weight equal to the damage it could bring. But it was lighter than I would have guessed. Warmer. I squinted down the sight and aimed the gun at the TV, wondering if I should trust John, if I really could pull the trigger and not riddle the living room drywall. I didn't have the guts to find out. Keeping all four fingers locked on the handle, I said, "Rat-a-tat" and passed the gun to Steve. He was unimpressed. He'd played with the UZI before.

"Wanna see more?" John said.

I didn't. But I nodded anyway.

He gave an exaggerated bow and gestured toward the garage. "Then I shall dip back into the cache."

For the next hour or so, until Steve and I finally retreated to our sleeping bags, John told one 'Nam assassination story after another.

As he talked, I laser-sighted empty pistols and pulled the pins on disarmed grenades. I was shit-scared handling these weapons, but I was worried that if I let it show, then John would think I was a pansy-assed peacenik who was afraid to get dirt under his nails. A guy like my dad.

***

John's UZI was the first thing that came to mind three years later, on a winter morning in my Ohio State dorm room, when a call from my mom woke me up. Her voice was shaky, phlegmy. She said that squad cars were lined along our street. From our front porch, she'd watched police lead John Parsons away in handcuffs.

Prosecutors alleged that John had set off a firebomb under the mobile home where a man named Michael Gustin was living. When Gustin fled the burning trailer, John, they said, was waiting outside with a 12 gauge Winchester. He allegedly shot Gustin twice. The state called for the death penalty. It was a revenge killing, the prosecution claimed, payback for an incident a few months earlier, when Gustin had accused John of breaking into the apartment Gustin was renting at the time. John insisted that he didn't break into the place, that it was a simple misunderstanding: He'd been hired by Gustin's landlord to do some maintenance work. He and Gustin argued, then fought, and in the scuffle John broke the man's ribs. Gustin apparently told friends he was afraid John would come back to kill him, so he moved out of the apartment and into the mobile home, where he'd be harder to find. He also threatened to file assault charges against John for the broken ribs. But John allegedly smoked him out and shot him down before Gustin had the chance.

From John's basement, police seized ten guns, including the UZI, the Winchester, and two homemade semi-automatics. They found silencers and grenade components. They found seventy-four containers of chemicals, more than enough materiel for an ex-science teacher to enact his own personal scorched earth policy.

Still I thought John was innocent. By then I was an eighteen-year-old political science major, and my worldview had widened enough to accommodate a healthy skepticism toward guys like John, big talkers who bragged about their glory days. Shortly after my dad moved out, he told me he didn't care much for John; he thought the guy was a blowhard, a bully. Now I understood that my dad had been right. John's tales from Vietnam were surely exaggerations, and, more likely, out-and-out lies. I didn't believe for a second that he'd sniped a Viet Cong general, and I didn't believe he was guilty of killing Michael Gustin or anybody else either. In fact, firebombing a mobile home and hiding in the bushes, waiting with a Winchester for the kill shot, seemed *exactly* like the kind of thing John would have gloated to Steve and me about, which, to my thinking, made it the last thing he would have actually done.

The alternative—that John really was a killer—was much harder to believe, despite the evidence. No way could the guy who taught me how to edge crown molding be a killer. No way had a killer spent so much time working in my house, or had I spent so much time hanging around his. Besides, he just didn't look like a murderer, any more than our Worthington street looked like a place where a murderer might live. With his big plastic glasses and paint-flecked coveralls, he looked exactly like what he was: a chemistry teacher, a doer of odd jobs. Perhaps most importantly, my mom insisted that John was innocent, that he was home watching movies with Steve on the night of the murder, just like he'd told the police. She knew John much better than I did, better than almost anyone did. She believed him, and I believed her. And their nightly dog walks continued, even with John out on bail, awaiting the trial that could send him to the electric chair.

***

The first installment of *The State of Ohio vs. John L. Parsons* ended in a hung jury. My mom was appalled that he wasn't simply found innocent and set free, but she was optimistic that the retrial would deliver the correct and just result. We all were. At the request of John's defense team, the second trial was conducted before a three-judge panel, rather than a traditional jury. This seemed a smart tactical move: put John's fate in the hands of professionals rather than schmucks off the street. But the three judges were unable to reach a unanimous agreement, so the deliberations were again declared hung. John would have to be tried a third time. "If two hung trials doesn't leave a *reasonable doubt*," my mom said, "I don't know what would."

At trial number three, the prosecutors finally got their man. The jury found John guilty of aggravated murder. My mom was sad but resigned, and she quickly girded up and set about enduring what she couldn't change. Instead of lamenting the verdict, she looked ahead to the penalty phase, wherein the jury would deliberate on whether John would be sentenced to life in prison or to death row and the chair.

John's lawyers called both my parents to testify as character witnesses. I wanted to go to the courthouse to watch my mom's testimony in person, but I had Poli Sci classes I couldn't cut, so I missed seeing her tell the jury about walking Rex with John and his dogs, about how he was always quick to help us fix things up. The next day, however, my dad was scheduled to appear, and with no classes, I took the bus downtown and found a seat in the courtroom gallery, nervous when they called him to the stand. I knew that he'd once testified in Washington before a congressional subcommittee, but that DC hearing had been about civil rights for the disabled, an issue I saw as mundane at the time. Here in Ohio the stakes were literally life and death. My dad was fiercely anti-capital punishment, so I was worried that he'd lie under oath, tell everyone how much he liked and respected John. Even worse, he might tell the truth, that he thought John was a loud-mouthed bully. I figured if my dad blew it, John would fry.

Sitting in the witness chair, my dad looked very much at ease. He answered the defense's questions in a voice clear and authoritative, turning his head to address the jurors directly. He told the court that John had taught me important lessons: the value of working with my hands, that treating a dog well demonstrated a respect for life. I sat there proud as hell, listening to my dad explain that John was an asset to the community, to the neighborhood, to our family, and it hit me that my dad was talking about the man who had, to some degree, replaced him. And he was saving that man's life.

The jury didn't buy it. They came back with a death recommendation. The judge, however, was swayed by the testimonials of my parents and others, and he made the controversial decision to go against the jurors and spare John by assigning the life sentence, no chance of parole for 39 years, when John would be 80. "John Parsons is unique," the judge was quoted in the paper as saying. "This man was an educator in our community, a good educator and an outstanding handyman. If a person has lived 41 years helping the old and young, that has to go for something."

The prosecution disagreed, of course. "John Parsons knew a lot of good people," the assistant prosecutor said. "But those people didn't know John Parsons. There was another side of John Parsons...John Parsons the destroyer."

***

John has spent the last twenty years transferring from one of Ohio's medium-security prisons to another. He's now assigned to the Marion Correctional Institution, having just moved up from

Chillicothe, where he spent the last several years locked up less than five miles from the house where my dad lives with my stepmom. John and my mom exchange letters every few months, and in those letters he seems better than stoic, almost happy. Lately he's been writing to tell her how proud he is of a prison program he started, teaching English to the Spanish-speaking inmates. He calls the students his Chihuahuas. They call him *El Perro Gordo*. The fat dog.

I'm now the same age John was on the day he was sentenced, and I still don't know for sure if he's guilty or innocent. Maybe guilt versus innocence is too simple a binary. I feel sad for the Gustin family, but I remember John fondly—murderer or not, braggart or not—and I doubt anything I could learn about him would change that. These days when I think of John, I don't picture him wearing an orange jumpsuit, sitting in a prison library, reading to Latino inmates. I don't even imagine him behind the wheel of the El Camino, ashing a Camel out the car window. Instead I remember a story my mom once told me about a particular night when I was in college and John was out on bail, waiting for his first trial.

On that night, my mom was awakened by hideous moans coming from outside her bedroom door. Worried that my sister might be sick, she shot out of bed and hurried down the hall to Jill's room. But now it was obvious that the wails weren't coming from my sister. These were animal noises, deep and desperate. She found Rex curled at the bottom of the stairs, panting, feverish, in agony. The dog couldn't walk. Her eyes were dull. My mom tried to stand Rex up, but the dog fell splay-legged to the floor. She felt Rex's belly and wondered if one of the fatty tumors had finally burst. As a nun, she'd often sat bedside. She knew when a body's time was up.

My mom wasn't strong enough to lift Rex, let alone carry the dog to the car. She sat on the stairs, head in hand, unsure of her next move. As the dog panted frantically, my mom rubbed her behind the ears, thinking back to the day when my dad carried Rex-the-stray-puppy home. Things were good then. Why wasn't he here to help now, when it might matter? Goddamn him for leaving her alone in this house to tend to cracked garage windows and dying dogs all by herself. Then she remembered something one of her Vietnamese ESL students had told her years before. The Vietnamese woman had been reading my mom's palm, when she curled her fingers closed, patted my mom on the back of the hand, and said, "You will always be taken care of."

So even though it was smack in the middle of the night, my mom called John. She told him Rex was dying. He got out of bed and, like always, came right over. He said he'd handle it. And he did. He put one arm under Rex's jaw and the other in the crook of her hind legs. He muscled her up to his chest and carried her out to the backyard. He loaded a pistol, one he'd apparently hidden from the police. He attached the silencer. He aimed the gun at the dog's head.

A single shot. Quiet as a cork pop. And as my mom cried in bed, as Worthington slept, John Parsons walked into my garage, pulled out the shovel, and started digging.

—2012

The Low Season

All you have to do is say no. That's the whole job. When the sales consultant leans back in his office chair, crosses his manicured fingers behind his head, and says, *So what do you think? Does this sound like something you might be interested in?* you just say no. One of you. Both of you. Somebody, for Christ's sake, say no. And you'll walk with 3,500 pesos. About 360 dollars. You'll have bought yourself twelve more days in lovely Puerto Vallarta.

But there's a catch. Saying no isn't as easy as it sounds. If saying no were simply a matter of spitting out those two letters, Uncle Sam would have won the war on drugs during the Reagan Administration. Saying no is tough duty. Especially when everything you see, the good Mexican coffee and buttery croissants, the glossy brochure and its four-color photos of "silken, sunlit beaches" and "polished blue waters," the pie charts and matrices and spreadsheets, even the legal pad with the sales consultant's pencil sketch of a Master Suite floor plan—everything laid out before you on this crystalline-topped table screams, yes!

These people are *yes* professionals. Every element of their presentation is designed to get a yes out of you, and for you to consummate that liberating, life-affirming yes, that sweet breath of freedom—ah, the relief and resignation that is *yes*—by signing here and initialing there and there and there and congratulations!

You'll want to say yes. You'll want to make the sales consultant happy, proud of you. You'll want to please him. *But you're doing this for you*, he'll tell you. *You deserve this.* And it would feel so good, so indulgently right, to say yes. You'd walk out of the office hand in hand like the happy couples in the brochure, and with the sales consultant gripping your shoulder, you'd look out the enormous plate-glass windows and—yes!—the sand *is* silken. Somehow you hadn't noticed this distinctly silky quality before. The Pacific *is* the color of . . . of . . . sapphires. The beach *is* lined with swaying palm trees, kissed by ocean breezes. Say yes and you'd ride back to your hotel, your plain, pedestrian hotel, looking ahead to a hundred years of luxury, lived two weeks at a time. Imagine it. The two of you. Not just guests, but denizens, no—owners!—of the world-class, the five-star, the very pinnacle of splendor, the Mayan Palace.

Then you'd fly back to Milwaukee or Akron or Rochester wondering how the hell—with your mortgage and car payments and a bitch of a heating bill—you're going to swing a $25,000 loan for a Mexican timeshare.

But what if I told you there was another way? A better way. What if I promised to share the secret to how you can fund a not-quite-luxury but still highly serviceable Mexican beach vacation?

It won't be entirely easy. You'll have to work for it. You'll have to say no. No matter what. That's the job.

So what do you think? Does this sound like something you might be interested in?

***

"Amigos!"

This is how it starts.

"Where you from, my friends?"

In Mexican resort towns, this is always how it starts.

"You from England? Canada? Germany?"

With a voice shouted from a six-foot wide, four-foot deep booth in the storefront stucco.

"You speak English? Parlez-vous Français? What, amigos, Deutsch?"

With the tout.

The booth is wallpapered with posters. Palm trees and jungle. Clear skies and sparkling water. A clean-cut Mexican guy sits on a makeshift wooden counter, painted a fresh coat of white. He's thumbing a scrapbook of guided-tour information. "You wanna go on a boat trip? Rent jet-skis? Go parasailing?"

He's about forty, and he's wearing a golf shirt and khakis. When he jumps to his feet, his boat shoes smack the cobblestones. Like many in this Pacific port of call, he speaks near-perfect English. And he makes his living from your vacation. "Come on, amigo. Where you from?"

"Ohio," I say, as my wife Kate and I skirt past him. We've been through this routine many times in the four days since we arrived in Puerto Vallarta. This is late September. The low season. An in-between time. Summer vacations have ended, and winter migrations are still being planned, existing only in cubicles, on computer screens, over water coolers. Kate and I have the *Plaza Principal* and the waterfront *Malécon* pretty much to ourselves. We don't have extra money for booze cruises or diving lessons, so we've said no to everything. Most of the touts now recognize us, the bald guy and the pretty brunette. They nod hello as we walk by, but they no longer bother with the sales pitch.

Not this guy. "Ohio, amigo?" he says. "My mother lives in Ohio."

This recognition of our home state stops us, turns us around. But I'm dubious. I wonder how many mothers he has. In how many states? How many countries?

"Lorain," he says. "You know it? Near Cleveland." This tout has either memorized the *Rand McNally* or he's telling the truth. He reaches for an album thick with Polaroids of sunburned *Norteam-ericanos* in scenes of organized, guided recreation—on horseback, behind snorkel masks. "Looks like fun, yes?"

"It does," I say. And I mean it. But I don't need to be reminded of all the fun Kate and I can't afford.

"When you decide you want to go, come and see me. Eyder.[1] Okay, amigo? I'll get you a good price."

"Very nice to meet you, Eyder," Kate says, nudging me forward. "But we've got to be going."

"How long are you in town, anyway?" Eyder says.

I look to the hills above Viejo Vallarta, where a blanket of haze settles on the trees, and I think, Well, amigo. That's complicated. Six weeks ago Kate and I moved out of our Columbus apartment, put all our furniture in storage, and loaded my rock band's Econoline with clothes and camping gear. The plan is to drive until the money runs out. Three months, maybe. Four if we scrimp. We spent the last six weeks tooling through the western United States, our cash supply bleeding through the van's shoddy transmission and 200,000-mile-old engine. Most nights we slept in the tent or crashed on floors, but we also treated ourselves to the occasional hotel room, knowing that because of our limited funds, one night in an American hotel—even a low-budget motel along the inter-state—would mean one less day at the end of our trip.

So here's the thing, amigo. You know the old cliché "time is money"? Our trip is governed by the inverse. For Kate and me, money is time. And now that we've made it here to beautiful—and, let's face it, cheap—Mexico, our financial outlook is improving. If we don't break the bank on the activities you're right now trying to sell us, we might be able to tap the nest egg for another month or so before pointing the van north and limping home.

I could say all of this to Eyder, this tout with a Buckeye for a mother, but I don't. I say, "We're not sure," and I extend my hand

1. Names in this essay have been changed.

toward him. We slide into that three-part handshake—first palms, then thumb webbings, then fingertips—of universal maleness. "See you around."

"Hang on, amigo," he says. "Where you staying?"

Playing in a band for twenty years has made me wary of this question. What I hear is, *Where will all your gear be parked tonight?* But I must have felt something trustworthy in the handshake, because I tell Eyder the truth. "Estancia San Carlos," I say, mentioning our $30 a night hotel by name. "Over on Constitución."

"That's a nice place," he says.

It is. The San Carlos is three stories of clean efficiencies wrapped around a bean-shaped pool. The apartment we're renting has a tiled living room and a functional kitchen with a refrigerator and propane-fueled stove. From the balcony, we see the green hills above and the yellow taxicabs below. In the evenings, Kate and I share a bottle of Mexican wine and watch the comings and goings of the cabbies lined up on Constitución. They crouch against a painted wall, facing the long row of their Nissan Tsuru taxis—the Mexican version of my own Sentra, which is currently parked in front of my mom's house, back in Columbus. They laugh and smoke and steal an occasional glance at Kate and me, the gringos up in the balcony. We've settled into a nice routine. So what if the apartment smells like propane? Who cares about a gas-leak headache when you're paying thirty bucks for a spot in paradise?

Now Eyder reaches into his back pocket and pulls out a brochure. "My friends," he says. "What are you doing tomorrow morning?"

Kate throws me a look that says, *Please, can't we just get dinner?*

I peel open the brochure. *The Mayan Palace.* For all the talk of snorkeling and bike tours, the touts are ultimately, always, working to get you to show up for a timeshare presentation. "Sorry, man," I say to Eyder. I take Kate's hand. "We're busy tomorrow morning."

This is not the truth. We have no plans for tomorrow. And surely Eyder suspects this. He knows that *busy tomorrow* probably means,

How much is the Mayan Palace willing to pay us? What's our time worth to them? Because, as Kate and I have learned, the resorts aren't afraid to sweeten the deal.

The question is how sweet.

***

Travel is always a combination of negotiation and compromise. Given the obstacles of language, laws, and customs, the traveler is subject to the push and pull of how he thinks things should work versus the reality of how they do—caught between what he wants and what he gets. This makes traveling different from vacationing. The vacationer spends hours researching the airfare, the hotel, the restaurants. Then he crosses his fingers that he'll make his connection in Atlanta, the weather won't suck, and the room will be as luxe as the Internet photos promise. Because of the built-in time constraints, the vacationer has little tolerance for the less-than-perfect. He wants to experience everything at its best. The traveler, however, either gets used to experiencing things as they (sometimes unfortunately) are or he doesn't have much fun. When ordering a whiskey and Seven in a foreign language, the traveler learns to smile and nod when the bartender pours him a tequila and Squirt. The traveler learns to say *close enough*. The traveler learns to enjoy the negotiation process, understanding that every exchange, win or lose, eventually becomes a meaningful part of the experience.

A week before this encounter with Eyder, Kate and I went on our first-ever timeshare presentation. We'd just crossed into Mexico at Nogales, headed for the resort town of San Carlos, when we were obliged to stop at a checkpoint to register the van with the Mexican authorities. A friendly young woman sitting at a card table offered to help us manipulate the bureaucratic maze. She told us which lines to stand in and which to avoid, and she sorted out which forms went to which official. Amid the stern-faced, gun-wielding *Fede-*

rales, her smile offered a much-appreciated *Bienvenidos á Mexico*. Then she asked the question Eyder would ask a week later: Where are you staying?

We didn't know yet. But we knew that wherever we stayed, it had to be cheap.

The woman held up a brochure. "If you want," she said, "you can stay three nights at this resort for free."

Kate and I looked at each other and shrugged. Cheap's good. Free's better.

The Sea of Cortez Premiere Vacation Club was clean and sterile in a Myrtle Beach Holiday Inn kind of way. The suites had ocean views and kitchenettes and were decked out in durable, guest-proof furnishings—plastic on plastic. Even white-washed of all character, it was a heck of a lot nicer than the Motel 6s and Super 8s we'd sprung for in the US. In order to get the room free of charge, we signed up to take a ninety-minute tour of the complex.

Kate and I met the Premiere Vacation Club sales guy at breakfast the next morning. He was from Southern California, and he wore a scraggy moustache that highlighted his hollow cheeks and pasty complexion. His face seemed carved by too many late nights and too few vitamins. Like the breakfast itself—watery eggs on chipped chinaware—this guy was one part optimism, two parts desperation.

"Here's the thing," he said. "I'm not into high pressure. I don't want to waste your time, and I don't want you to waste mine. So before I even start my pitch, tell me if you're interested. You say yes, and we'll keep talking. You say no, and I'll let you get back to the beach."

We said no. And he didn't argue or backpedal or even try to flip us to a maybe. He just clicked his ballpoint into his shirt pocket, gathered his charts and graphs, and invited us to help ourselves to more of the breakfast buffet.

Twenty minutes later Kate and I were lounging under an umbrella made of braided palm fronds. It had been too easy. I never

got to unholster my ruthless bargaining powers. As the desert sun
climbed and the tide rolled in, we lifted ourselves from our towels only to reposition our deck chairs and adjust the angle of our
umbrella, to negotiate the boundary between sand and sea, between
sun and shade.

***

This is how Eyder makes his living: Properties like the Mayan
Palace, The Plaza Pelicanos Grand Beach Resort, and Krystal International Vacation Club hire him to track down married couples
willing to sign up for the tour. Eyder knows that nobody wants
to waste hard-earned vacation time sitting through a sales pitch.
He's used to the brush-off. But he has a wife and kids. He has bills
to pay and school uniforms to buy, so like all the touts, he hustles.
He's always on the job. When shopping at Wal-Mart, he looks for
gringos who need help finding the Coppertone or the Pepto. He
points Mr. and Mrs. Norteamericano in the right direction, and
then he reaches for the brochure in his back pocket.

How much money does Eyder pull in for every couple he delivers
to the mega-resorts lining Banderas Bay? I don't know. But when
Kate and I tell him we're busy tomorrow morning, and we couldn't
possibly visit the Mayan Palace, he tells us that the hotel can offer
us 3,500 pesos for taking the ninety-minute tour.

"*Thirty-five hundred* pesos?" I say in genuine amazement. "Are
you serious?" My internal accountant, so intimate with the red pencil, sharpens the virgin black pencil, dons the eyeshade, and goes to
work. Thirty-five hundred pesos at a 10.48 peso-to-dollar exchange
is about 360 dollars—or ten percent of our budget for this entire
months-long trip. If the Estancia San Carlos is costing us thirty
bucks a night, this means we'd be trading ninety minutes at the
Mayan Palace for twelve more nights at the San Carlos. The Mayan
Palace would be *paying* us to stay somewhere else. There must be a
catch. "Thirty-five hundred in *cash*?"

Eyder laughs and says, "*Sí*. Of course, amigo. You have a nice breakfast. You take the tour. Then they'll give you the money." He pretends to stack bills one by one into my open palm. "If you want to buy, that's fine, but if you say no and take the cash, that's fine too. I don't care. Just as long as you show up."

I try to suss out the economics of the system. The Mayan Palace must give Eyder a budget of, say, 4,000 pesos to spend on each couple. Then maybe he keeps the difference between the total budget and what it costs him to lure prospective buyers, in this case 3,500, leaving him a profit of 500. But can the Mayan Palace really afford to gamble 4,000 pesos, more than 400 dollars, on the purchasing whims of every couple? If so, folks would have to say yes a whole lot of the time. The resort must have the success rate of a Mayo Clinic surgeon.

But if I'm right about how the system works, why did Eyder start at 3,500 pesos instead of 2,500 or even 1,500? Maybe he's a volume dealer. Small margin, heavy traffic. But I'm worried about the more likely scenario, that Eyder's cut is totally independent of the incentive the Mayan Palace offers tourists like us. The resort probably just kicks him a hundred pesos or so for every couple he drags in.

I look down at his boat shoes—the mud-caked leather and thin soles—and hope he makes a good living peddling timeshare tours. That he can support his family, visit his mom in Ohio, take a vacation himself every now and then.

No. That's not it. I hope he's *soaking* the Mayan Palace *and* the suckers who buy timeshares there. I hope Eyder lives in one of those white houses up in the hills, like the one I can see this very moment, jutting through the trees, painted orange by the sunset. I wince at the thought of Eyder working night and day funneling gringos through a five-star resort only to squeeze his family into one of the concrete-walled apartments that line Route 200 on the edge of town.

"You have a credit card?" Eyder says. He's reaching into a portfolio for the official Mayan Palace invitation form.

"Well, yeah," I say. "But what do we need it for? They're paying *us*, right?"

"Don't worry, amigo." Eyder taps a Bic pen against the form, leaving a patch of tiny moons on the carbon sheet. "They just want to look at it. They won't charge you for anything." And then he hands me the form. He aims the pen at the line where he has written *3,500 pesos*.

Can Kate and I even consider taking $360 for our time if in fact Eyder makes only a few dollars a day for his? Is our time worth more than Eyder's just because we're the ones with the MasterCard?

Then again, the cash is going to end up with somebody; it might as well be us. And it's not like we're stealing from Eyder. This is the Mayan Palace's money.

So yeah. Of course we can take it. We *have* to take it. We'd be fools not to.

"That's the deal, amigos," he says. "3,500 pesos. Ninety minutes. You want to do it?"

Hell yes we do.

***

Should you decide to go into the business of working the time-share system for cash, you need to meet a few qualifications. It's not like the Mayan Palace just hands out money to any knucklehead that drifts in off the beach. First, you've got to be married, with passports to prove you have the same last name. And husband and wife must show up for the tour together. The sales staff isn't about to go through the whole spiel getting you to sign on the line, only to have your wife nix the deal when you stand in the doorway, arms spread wide, and say, *Hey, honey. Guess what we just bought?*

Second, you need to be packing that almighty credit card. If so, then the Mayan Palace figures you've already been vetted and you've established a credit record they can dig up later. Asking you to flash your MasterCard is a quick way to gauge your purchasing power, and it seems more tasteful and less intrusive than running your full credit report. Nothing would kill the yes vibe like subjecting you to a credit screening over Denver omelets.

Third...there is no third. Married with credit cards. That's pretty much it. Eyder's got the green light to make the invite.

Oh sure, the invitation form does contain a few fine print items. There's something in there about being ineligible if you've taken another timeshare tour in the previous seven days. And don't bother showing up if you plan on staying in Mexico for more than two weeks. And if you're a student? Walk your impoverished ass back to the hostel, amigo. The Mayan Palace ain't interested. Their ideal prospects are white-collar professionals who grind for fifty weeks and vacation for two. The restrictions are meant to weed out couples like Kate and me, folks who, although pretty much broke, would quit their jobs, put their crap in storage, and spend most of their savings on a trek through Mexico. The six-point font caveats are safeguards against *travelers* blemishing the finely manicured grounds.

But remember: Eyder needs you to show up. So he's not in the disqualification business. When you answer that yes, you are in fact a student, he'll write "Teacher" on the form next to the word *Occupation*. When you tell him that you've been in Mexico for a week, and you plan on staying for at least another month, and maybe two, he'll enter "One" on the line next to *Weeks in Mexico*. And he'll just ignore you when you try to tell him the story of your previous timeshare presentation at The Sea of Cortez Premiere Vacation Club.

Next, Eyder will coach you. He'll explain exactly how to answer should these questions come up in the presentation itself. Then he'll tell you not to worry, they probably won't ask anyway. They'll be too busy selling.

When Eyder finally rips off the invitation form and hands it to you, he says, *Okay, amigos. Tomorrow morning. Ten o'clock.* He knows you might forget. Or oversleep. Or change your mind. But Eyder leaves nothing to chance. He's invested too much in you. He won't let you forget or oversleep or change your mind.

Before you walk away, Eyder will give you a thumbs up and an almost imperceptible wink. Your old concert t-shirt and ripped jeans are a clear sign that you can't afford an upscale timeshare. But he doesn't care. His job is to get you there.

***

The next morning, the hotel phone rings. I look across the horizon of the bed, over Kate's shoulder, toward her travel alarm: 9:32. The ringing has temporarily silenced the debate between Kate and me over whether to follow through on this presentation or not. She wants to collect the money and get it over with. I want to sleep off my hangover and re-book for this afternoon. I reach for the phone. "Hola?"

"Señor, Joe! Buenas dias!" says a clearly not hungover Eyder. "Ready for the tour?"

"You said ten o'clock, right?"

"The tour *starts* at ten."

Kate slides out of bed and heads to the bathroom. I sit up too quickly, and the headache settles into my frontal lobe. Massaging my temples, I stretch the phone cord out to the balcony. Two cabbies are parked along the curb, smoking cigarettes under a tree. "How long does it take to get there by taxi?" I say.

"No, Señor Joe. I'm in the lobby. Waiting for you."

"You're downstairs right now?"

"Come down whenever you're ready."

I hang up, and I can hear Kate knocking her toothbrush against the sink. "Remember, this was all your idea," she says. She rinses and spits. "You wanted to talk to the guy. I wanted to get dinner."

She's right, of course. And when we finally did walk away from Eyder to go eat, I was still trying to sell her. "We can't afford *not* to do this," I said. We were sitting across the restaurant table from each other. "I mean, the gig pays $120 an hour." I dipped a chip into guacamole. "Each."

"If you're so worried about money," she said, "why'd you quit your job?"

"I quit my *day* job." I scanned the menu. "My *job* is playing music."

Kate smoothed her napkin across her lap. "And how much does that pay?"

Everything and nothing.

Like so many suburban kids, my career plan was to become a rock star. Unlike most suburban kids, rock stardom almost happened for me. Back in high school, my buddies and I formed a band we'd eventually call Watershed, and later, in our mid-twenties, we signed a six-figure deal with Epic Records. We moved from Ohio into a Manhattan apartment. We spent our major label money on studio time and producers' fees. We downed Heineken and sushi at parties where industry-types cupped their hands to our ears and whisper-shouted that we were the next big thing. But after our debut album didn't sell, the label dropped us.

Ten years have passed since we lost the Epic deal, and though Watershed has had plenty of success over the last decade—maintaining a steady following, writing songs that have been played on Columbus radio stations—none of that success is reflected in my bank account. I can't afford to quit my day job. But before Kate and I packed up the van and aimed for Mexico, that's exactly what I did.

I'd been working as an admin at an architecture firm, which was just my latest stab at finding an acceptable, bill-paying plan B. I've also supervised a sheltered workshop for the disabled. I've bussed tables and washed dishes. I've served up meatloaf to murderers in a psychiatric hospital. I've driven trucks and forklifts. I've bagged groceries and rounded up shopping carts. I've taken the LSAT and applied to law schools. I've thought seriously about joining the CIA.

Rock and roll used to afford me the delusion of certainty. In my teens and twenties, I was utterly convinced I'd end up a famous musician. Even after being dropped from Epic, I was still certain the music career would work out—at least well enough to pay the rent. But now, as I slide into to my mid-thirties, I can't help but doubt a little. And that doubt is reinforced every time Kate and I get invited to our non-musician friends' houses for dinner, and we see their soaring ceilings and chef's-grade kitchens, their crown molding and Jacuzzi tubs, their wine refrigerators and rumpus rooms. Kate and I clearly aren't as successful as commercials and sit-coms tell us we should be at our age. So I fall back on the position that material wealth is—to borrow Terry Southern's phrase—nothing but "flash and filigree." I tell myself that my by-the-book friends are anesthetized by their possessions, that their Sony flat screens and TiVo boxes and Harman Kardon home theater systems are mere table scraps the people with real power serve up as distractions. *Let them eat name-brand consumer electronics!*

Until recently Kate also felt this pressure to measure up to our friends—and to the image of thirty-something success that our friends represent. A few years ago, back when she was working sixty hours a week for a hip ad agency and before I'd taken the position at the architecture firm, she would come home late, collapse on our ratty couch, look around our college-ghetto apartment, and give me a look that said, *You're gonna have to get a real job soon, buddy.* But these days she's a full time PhD student in British Literature. She makes a quarter of the money she used to, and yet she's more comfortable in our apartment—and in our friends' houses—than I am. She seems content with what little we own; she's not bothered by the many things we don't. Or maybe she's just too busy writing 25-page analyses of Victorian novels to indulge in the anxiety and envy that I'd been feeling in the months before we started this trip.

Right now Kate's looking into the bathroom mirror, applying her lip gloss. Satisfied, she turns to me. "Okay, amigo," she says.

She's got my toothpaste in one hand, my toothbrush in the other.
"Time to go to work."

***

Eyder's dented Nissan bolts through the streets of Old Town. I'm
sitting up front with him, and Kate's alone in the back. We speed past
cart vendors shouting, *Bebidas! Frescos!* and kids in starched-stiff
school uniforms—laughing boys with clip-on ties and cool girls with
white knee socks. Wiry men in work boots emerge from hardware
stores fronted with spools of rope and chain. Eyder is telling me that
he used to manage a restaurant but quit that job to work as a tout.
The pay is better. He downshifts to pass a slow-moving pick-up, and
the painted store signs streak kaleidoscopic in my peripheral vision.

Kate rolls down her window. In the sideview mirror, I see her
face. Pretty. Determined. I crank my window down too. Now I'm
closer to the people, to the sounds, to the wisps of image that will
settle in my memory. These are the souvenirs Kate and I will bring
home from our travels. But as Eyder hustles us from angular, street-
level Viejo Vallarta toward curvilinear, towering Nuevo Vallarta,
I keep this in mind: we're not traveling anymore. We're working.
We're here to conduct a simple transaction—time for money. We're
here to say one word and one word only.

Eyder hands us off to Steve, the sales pro who will serve as emis-
sary of the Mayan Palace. Then he steers the Nissan around the
resort's circular driveway, waving goodbye out the window.

I already miss Eyder. I'd started to feel a real bond with him.
We're co-conspirators, both in it for the cash, our motives neatly
aligned. The thirtyish Steve, with his open collar and fat stainless
watch, is in it for the money too, but it's *our* money he's after, just
as we are out for his. Motives colliding.

Now Eyder is speeding back to Old Town, and for the next ninety
minutes every Mexican we see will be at our service in some way—
pushing a dish cart, filling a water glass, cutting the Bermuda grass.

***

Steve leads us through the lobby, explaining that he recently moved to Puerto Vallarta from Vegas. He has the look of a croupier, of a man used to settling debts—slick hair, silk shirt. He goes out of his way to tell us he's not a salesman. "We don't need salesmen here," he says, smiling, "because these properties sell themselves." He stops. Turns to me. "I like to think of myself as an *educator*, Joe. Here to help you make an informed decision."

Kate says she's impressed by how tasteful the décor is. And there is something in the understated elegance of the lobby—streamlined, restrained, in stark contrast to the salt-water-taffyness of the Premier Vacation Club—that is truly impressive.

I'm staring over Steve's shoulder at an enormous black pool. I wonder aloud why nobody's swimming on such a nice day.

"That's a *reflecting* pool," Steve says. "Just for decoration." He lets out a chuckle and starts walking again. "We've got two *swimming* pools down by the beach."

I look at Kate and mouth the words: *reflecting pool*?

"But, hey," Steve says, turning toward us, walking backward. "There's no sense just talking about it. How about I show you instead?"

I check my watch. Ninety minutes…starts…now. Seven minutes to load up the complementary breakfast plates (two minutes each for the omelet and carving stations, two minutes to run through the buffet, and one to order juice and coffee). Twenty minutes to chew and swallow. Ten minutes for coffee refills and extra croissants. Five minutes to stroll back toward the residential area. Fifteen minutes for the explanation/demonstration of different room types (Master Room/Suite/Master Suite). Ten minutes to discuss the pros and cons of buying the optional golf package (spoiler alert: there aren't any cons). Fifteen minutes to walk back to poolside, stopping to check out the various gourmet dining and boutique shopping options. And then we're sitting in Steve's office, and he's leaning back in his chair asking, "So what do you think? Does this sound like something you might be interested in?"

There's a reason attorneys coach witnesses to answer with the fewest number of words possible: the more complex an explanation, the more holes you leave open. We should answer Steve with a firm *No, thanks. No* sucks the energy from the exchange. *No* is a knuckleball.

But instead of saying no, I twist my face and look up at the ceiling. "Well, you know … we're just … um … the thing is … we're not sure." Then I look toward Kate, finally landing on what feels to me like a solid protest. "What I'm saying is, we can't afford it right now."

We can't afford it is a bush league fastball right down the pike, a pitch Steve can mash. He springs forward in his chair and flips open a legal pad. "Don't be sure about that, Joe," he says. He's drawing a diagram that looks like the USDA food pyramid. "How many weeks do you vacation per year?"

I remember the fine print on Eyder's form. I don't want to slip and say something that will disqualify us from the cash, but at the same time I want to tell him, *Listen, pal. We don't vacation, okay. We travel. For months at a time. So this whole stinking bourgeois-yuppie resort deal isn't exactly our bag of beans.*

Instead, I say, "About two weeks."

Steve writes *two weeks* on the pad. "And how much do you spend on vacations every year?"

This is another opportunity to stand up and say, *Steve, buddy, seriously. We're not interested. We're trying to see the real Mexico. What's the point of coming here if you never leave the compound? So take the Cartier boutique and the reflecting pool back to Vegas. We'll take the pesos and be on our way.*

But for some reason, I can't be this blunt, not even to a stranger. I'm not sure why, but I'd feel guilty taking the money without letting Steve go through his spiel. I turn toward Kate. "What do you think? A couple thousand dollars, maybe?"

Steve laughs. "And you're telling me you can't *afford* this place?"

We're interrupted by Steve's leggy assistant, who offers us more good coffee. I take a sip. "I don't think it's really about the money," I say.

Steve pops open a Diet Coke. "You know, Joe and Kate, you guys have the right attitude. It's not about the money, is it? It's about *lifestyle*. It's about improving your *quality of life*." He crosses a black loafer over his knee. "That's where the Mayan Palace fits in. And ownership here is more affordable than you'd think."

I don't see how that's possible, but just to be sure I look down to Steve's legal pad, trying to see if he's scribbled a price anywhere. Nope. Just pie charts and pyramids. And a circular something that might be the Mayan calendar.

"Let me show you what I mean," he says. "How much do you spend per night on hotels?"

Here we've got him. "About thirty," I say.

"Wow," he says. "Thirty bucks?" He's a little stunned. I've shaken him, brushed him back. "Honestly, I don't know if I can make the numbers work after all." He goes nose-deep into the legal pad, trying to get his rhythm back. "Jeez, man. Thirty? What kind of places do you stay in? Hostels?"

"More like cheap hotels, I guess."

"*Exactly* like cheap hotels," Kate says. "Because when we go to a foreign country, we want to get a feel for the place. And if we stayed in a huge complex like this, I'm not sure we'd get that—"

"Local color," Steve says, shooting two pointer fingers at Kate. "That's cool, guys. I get it." He's back on *terra firma*. "I used to do that whole backpack thing. You know, hop on a train? Eurail Pass and a baguette?" He's nodding his head. Sitting up straight. "And that's fine when you're a kid, right? But you've gotta think about the

Kate and Joe of fifteen or twenty years down the road." He's rolling now, picking up speed, working toward his money line. "Trust me. There's gonna be a time in your life when you want a little more stability. You'll have had all the local color you can stand." And then he stops. Leans back in the chair. Looks me right in the eye. "You're gonna want to stay someplace nice."

I do want to stay someplace nice. I'm thinking of our apartment at the Estancia San Carlos: the snug balcony, the huge kitchen, the mosaic-tiled bathroom. But then I smell the exhaust from the taxis lined up on Constitución. I taste the propane leak. I feel the crunch of the fat cockroach that nearly tackled me in the shower the other morning, the one I killed and didn't tell Kate about.

"Yeah, man," Steve says. "Hostels. I used to dig 'em. Believe me. But now I'm thirty-two." He taps his finger on the brochure, on the Master Suite floor plan. "And I own *three* of these units…"

I think about the hotel in Tepic where we stayed two weeks ago. The shower mold. The fist-holes in the drywall.

"…understand, Kate and Joe. Ownership in the Mayan Palace is a lifetime investment. Your *kids* will inherit this place…"

I see the bare light bulb dangling over the chintz bedspread at the hotel in Los Mochis.

"…doesn't matter if you golf or not. The demand for golf packages is so huge, you can sell your weeks to a broker for twice what you paid…"

I hear the wild dogs gnashing outside our hotel window in Creel.

"…so you rent your unit to somebody else for one week, right? That pays for your second week. You get to vacation for *free*…"

Suddenly I want Steve to understand that we probably could afford a unit at the Mayan Palace if we flipped priorities just a bit. Because strangely, I don't want him to be, I don't know, *disappointed*, I guess. But in what? Kate and me as consumers? This is absurd, obviously, but still, I want Steve to feel optimistic about us.

And about Eyder's ability to dig up prospects like us. I want Steve to feel good about himself, to be content with his life, even if I'm not exactly satisfied with mine.

"Kate. Joe," Steve says. "This deal is a money *maker.*" He's got his palms flat on the desk. He's down to brass tacks. "Honestly, and this is just me talking now, but I don't see how you can afford *not* to do it."

I don't want to disappoint Steve, it's true. But more importantly, I don't want to disappoint myself. I don't want to disappoint Kate. If we could somehow work out the money, if we could scratch together a down payment, if we could just give in to that all-powerful and ever-living yes, it would signal to us and everyone else that Kate and I had *succeeded.* Instead of measuring our success in a slippery concept like "freedom," we could point to a tangible asset, brochure-worthy proof of the prosperity our working lives had bought us. The payments wouldn't be so bad. Couple hundred bucks a month. Sure I'd have to find a proper job when we got back to Ohio, and I'd certainly have to cut back on my time with the band, but aren't these the compromises successful adults make?

Maybe at thirty-four I've finally figured out that being an adult *means* balancing freedom and responsibility. Steve is offering us the chance to take ownership not just in a timeshare but in our own adulthood. And, yeah, he's right: We probably will have kids some-day. Do we really want to drag them into a roach den? Wouldn't it be lovely to just laze by the pool, watching the little guys splash around while we flag down the waiter for another bucket of Coronas? Seriously, why do Kate and I always have to work so hard, with so little to show for it? Don't we deserve nice things?

Yes.

Yes we do.

Kate and I deserve this.

And here's Kate. She's smiling. She's been thinking the same thing. Now she'll chime in with the *yes* that'll make everybody happy.

But she's scooting her chair away from the desk. She's leaning over for her purse. She's saying, "Steve, thanks so much for taking the time to talk to us. The resort is truly beautiful, but right now, where Joe and I are in our lives, it's just not a good fit." She stands up, slides the brochure back to him. "So our answer is no."

Steve winces. He looks like he just rimmed out a four-foot birdie putt.

"Now, if you'll please excuse us," Kate says, "we've got to be going."

***

The Mayan Palace won't let you walk without a fight. It's not like you say no and everyone instantly breaks character, the confetti comes raining down, and two *Price-Is-Right* models slide out from behind a curtain to hand you a giant check. You don't say no just once; you've got to drive the point home like a railroad spike.

Say no to Steve, then you wrangle with his boss, who explains the whole deal again in painstaking detail, down to the food pyramid and the Mayan calendar. *Did Steve explain that you can sell your extra weeks? And you know about the golf packages?*

Disarm the bossman with a string of *no-no-nos*, and you're steered outside to a lush veranda, where you're force-fed more coffee, then left under the trellis to contemplate your flawed decision.

After fifteen minutes, a third sales guy comes out. Steve's boss's boss. *El* motherfucking *Jefe*. He looks like the other two, but older, balder. He runs through the particulars yet again. *You do understand that this is a money-making opportunity, correct? What if I were to tell you that just for today we were running a special?*

No the big boss to death and you're almost home. All that's left is a half-hearted spiel from the guy who's trying to unload the pre-owned units. *These suites here are just like new, but at half the price, see? You and I both know you can afford one of these.*

Finally you convince him that he can't say anything that will change your mind. Nothing. Nada. No.

"Walk through that door over there," he says, slumping ever-so-slightly. "They'll get you your money."

And that's where the five-star hospitality ends.

In the business office, you're scowled at by a woman who's Department of Motor Vehicles–surly. She opens the cash drawer and counts out seven 500-peso notes, evil-eying you as if it were her own personal money. She doesn't say *Thank you* or *Goodbye*. She doesn't point you to the exit. You're left to wander the lobby in search of the driveway where you last saw Eyder.

When you walk through the front doors and into the Pacific sun, even the bellhops and valets seem vaguely disappointed in you. Nobody blows a whistle to hail you a cab, so you wave toward the line-up of blue and white Nissans. One of the taxis breaks rank and circles the driveway, and you reach into your wallet, hoping you have enough small bills to get back to Old Town. You didn't realize you'd be paying for the ride home.

As Kate and I squeeze into the cab, I'm regretting what might have been, heavy with *non*-buyer's remorse. But the magnetic pull of the Mayan Palace is weakened with every mile the taxi puts between it and us. When we jerk to a stop at the simple and charming and 99% cockroach-free Estancia San Carlos, it seems ridiculous that I'd been so tempted—ridiculous because it wasn't the condos themselves that had seduced me. It wasn't the 1,200 thread-count linens or the brushed-aluminum fridge and granite countertops. The luxury isn't what I wanted. That stuff is just fabric. Just metal and rock. Sure, I suppose I wished we could afford the Mayan Palace, but what I really wanted was to say no to it. I wanted to walk away convinced that Kate and I didn't need a swank time-share to validate our lives.

But I didn't say no. Kate did. She stuck to the plan. She did the job.

—2007

The Bodyman

1. The Thousand-Dollar House

Dave Cook is staying in tonight. He's come down with whatever flu virus has been going around. But that's not why he's staying in. "Sick" is just not that big a deal to Dave. He's been sick every day for forty-two years. He was born with Wilson's disease, a rare genetic disorder that has damn-near killed him several times over. So, no, Dave is not staying in because he's sick. He's staying in because, as he says, "I don't look too sweet, and I smell like shit, and I ain't taking a fucking shower." Dave ain't taking a fucking shower because he doesn't have a shower. He doesn't have running water or indoor plumbing. Yet. For now he washes himself with Gojo hand cleaner dispensed from a gallon-sized container, and he rinses with the rainwater and snowmelt he's collected in buckets out back. To take an actual hot-running-water shower, Dave has to track down T-Bone. T-Bone's got a shower. But T-Bone doesn't have a phone. Finding him is usually more of a hassle than it's worth, so Dave keeps a stash of clean underwear and socks in a plastic grocery bag. Beyond that, he wears the same thing nearly every day, whether he's welding a resonator under a buddy's LeSabre or working the cash register at Cloud Nine Pipes and Stuff: Carhartt overalls, an old sweatshirt, a Rip Curl skullcap. He looks a bit like a young, thin Jack Nicholson circa *One Flew Over the Cuckoo's Nest*, but this get-up doesn't necessarily fly at most of Columbus, Ohio's hotter nightspots. So Dave Cook is staying in tonight.

At Dave's house, one's conception of "in" must be reassessed. "In" typically suggests a certain degree of structural integrity, enough to ensure that whatever is "out"—the wind, the cold, the neighbors—stays out. But on this February night, Dave's house is penetrable by one and all. The walls of what will soon be his living room consist of nothing but aluminum siding and plywood—no insulation, no drywall, no paint. To keep from freezing to death, Dave fires up a kerosene space heater that's loud as a jet engine. When it gets so cold that even this heater is out-gunned, he retreats to the back bedroom, an eight-by-eight-foot nook that he recently finished draping with pink fiberglass. The bedroom is cordoned off from the living room by a ratty blanket that hangs from the ceiling, and thanks to the new insulation and a smaller electric heater, it's comparatively luxurious back there.

This house, which Dave has dubbed Cook Acres, is the first major item he has owned that doesn't have wheels, and it's his only because he was lucky enough to know a guy, who knew a guy, who knew that the previous owner had died and left the property to his deadbeat, meth-addict of a son. The son then let the house rot—literally *rot*— in a four-foot swamp of standing water in the basement. Looking to get out from under the dilapidation and the property taxes, and clearly more focused on his addiction than on his deceased father's old house, the meth-head decided to see what he could get for the place. That's when Dave and a lawyer friend made the kid an offer: one thousand dollars. A grand. For a house on a wooded half-acre. Dave paid less for a home than you'd pay for a rusted-out used car at one of the *buy-here, pay-here* lots in his neighborhood. You could pay more, a lot more, for a new bicycle.

Dave Cook—*landowner*—then gave away his old pad, a shabby mobile home that had been up on blocks in an urban trailer park, to a girlfriend who was riding rough over a stretch of bad luck. He and his dog, Cole, would bunk out in the garage at the new house until he and a crew of buddies finished gutting the living areas.

This project would last several months. The floors were rotten and needed to be ripped out and replaced. Walls had to come down. The entire ceiling support system needed to be rebuilt, and—most important if Dave and Cole were to survive the frigid Ohio winter—insulation had to be hung.

Work on those short days was slow going, and the week before Christmas, when an Alberta Clipper blew over the Great Lakes and left Columbus coated in a quarter-inch of ice, Dave and Cole were still sleeping in the garage. On Christmas Eve, the temperature dipped so low that Dave feared for his life. He worried that before he could move into the house-proper, the purchase of which signified one of the few genuine lucky breaks he'd ever had, he would slip away, frozen in a death grip with his Shepherd mix. Dave made a pact with Cole that night: If Dave froze first, Cole should just go ahead and eat him. If Cole was first to succumb, Dave would not only eat the dog but also skin him and wear him as a coat. It's difficult to know if Cole harbored any resentment toward Dave for the mental leap to dog-as-winter-coat, but a few weeks later when the garage caught fire, Cole must have either forgiven or forgotten, because upon the first whiff of deadly smoke, the dog barked and howled like a citified Lassie, waking up Dave just minutes before the flames reached the tanks of compressed oxygen and acetylene—welding supplies—that would have blown them both into the January night.

Now the half-charred garage has been added to the rehabilitation project that is Dave's life. But Cook Acres is coming together. The floor is laid down, the power hooked up, the first few swatches of precious insulation hung. And man and dog have moved into the main house. Life for Dave Cook is as good as it has ever been.

***

The DJ on the classic rock station says it's eighteen degrees, so Dave and I are in the warmer back bedroom. Rusty nails and loose staples are scattered in the sawdust and ash on the plywood floor. I'm sitting on a plastic folding chair with grooves the size of cigarette butts melted into the seat. Dave drops into a wicker Papasan, and every few sentences he looks warily at the old Radio Shack cassette recorder that sits on the floor between us. Even in the unforgiving glare of a halogen work lamp, Dave is staggeringly handsome. His jaw is comic-book hero square. He's on the muscular side of wiry, his muscles the hard-fought type that can only be built from physical labor. His is a body built for loosening rusted bolts and stuck lug nuts. A body built for generating torque.

The first time I met Dave, he was sitting on the curb in front of a sorority house, waiting for a ride. It was 1992, and Watershed was shopping for a cheap van to get us from Columbus to gigs in Louisville, Cleveland, Pittsburgh. My bandmates and I were all twenty-three and hopelessly ignorant of the greasy chess game that is the used vehicle market. Luckily our guitarist's little sister had a boyfriend who knew cars. He was a bodyman at a Cadillac dealership, a guy who pulled dents and hung side panels, and he had volunteered to come along to make sure we didn't get screwed by some shyster who would look at us and see three suburban kids with deep pockets. But as we pulled up to the Alpha Gamma Delta house, I saw that we weren't picking up just any gear-head. We were picking up Dave Cook, the neighborhood bully who had once lived a few houses down from me in faux-colonial Worthington. Dave Cook, owner of a Cobra with flames painted on the side, a car that had left skid marks and rainbow-slick puddles of Quaker State on our street. As a high schooler, I could have thrown a baseball from my porch to his, but we had never met. When I was sixteen, he was twenty-one. I was taking AP classes and he was ... well, I don't know what he was doing. But if the chatter on the basketball courts was true, it was Dave Cook those police helicopters had been looking for, their spotlights slicing through my backyard, the sound of their rotor blades reverberating in my pillow.

Dave has a DNA-level understanding of how machines work. In the fifteen years since he helped me buy a used van, I've seen him take a six-cylinder engine apart and put it back together in running order. I've watched him install brake rotors and set the choke on carburetors. He's also tarred roofs, plumbed kitchens, poured concrete. Most of Dave's work is done off the clock, favors for friends or for *friends* of friends. And even though he's the poorest guy I know, he steadfastly refuses to accept money as payment. He once built a roof over my mom's back deck and wouldn't take anything but a few home-cooked meals. After the roof went up, he cleaned my mom's gutters and mowed her lawn. Then he patched holes in her attic to keep the squirrels from eating the insulation. Just last month he installed an alternator in my piece-of-shit Sentra. For two hours, work on Cook Acres ceased as Dave went shoulder-deep into my car. Like always, he did this without hesitation and 100 percent pro bono, his only complaint aimed at the Japanese for making their alternators such pains in the ass to get to. This is typical Dave: A few years ago, when Watershed was touring through deep Mississippi, the van started spewing blue smoke. From the tailpipe. From under the hood. We sputtered to a pay phone and called him for a long-distance diagnosis. What he said after hello was, "Give me ten hours, and I'll be there."

Dave's voice is Marlboro-mellow. He speaks slowly and deliberately. But tonight his words are smothered by phlegmy sinuses, and he's slurring so badly that he's adding extra syllables. "Joe" comes out "Joe-oh." "People" sounds like "Pee-ee-ple." Later I'll have to rewind the tape over and over to figure out exactly what he's said. Now, as he works to crack open a carton of cigarettes, his hands tremble through the simple routine they've finished ten thousand times before. If I didn't know better, I'd say all the dope Dave smokes has finally dulled his motor skills. But that's not why Dave seems like such a burnout tonight. He seems like a burnout because his body is betraying him. And because it's been almost two months since he's taken the medicine that keeps him from dying.

Dave's access to the meds is tied to the waxing and waning of his finances, and when his wallet is especially thin, he can make a month's worth of pills last a year. At four bucks a pop, he sometimes can't afford the pills at all, and he might go six months without medication. Dave muscles through these stretches without complaint, refusing to acknowledge any ground gained by his illness, not willing to concede even a minor defeat. This winter he has a fairly large stash, but he can't take the medicine until he has access to a shower, to some means of cleaning himself other than with fistfuls of Gojo.

See, this particular medication saves Dave's life by flushing excess copper from his bloodstream and converting it to waste that is expelled via his routine bodily functions. That's how it's supposed to work, anyway—with tidy words like *expelled* and *routine*. But this is the reality: when Dave takes his meds, he shits and pisses himself. His body surrenders and opens up, shitting and pissing out the poison with no concern for cleanliness or decorum or for whether T-Bone happens to be at home. The very medicine that keeps Dave alive strips him of his dignity and reduces him from man to boy. Turns him back into a shitbag of a little kid who literally can't pee straight. It's enough to make a man beg for an exit strategy, to get down on his forty-two-year-old knees and say, "Jesus Christ, I'm having a hard time dealing with this shit. So come kill me, motherfucker. If you want it that bad, stop fucking with me. Let's get it done."

2. The Copper Repository

Dave Cook is a minister's son. Back in Granby, Connecticut, when Dave was twelve, his dad was busy serving the spiritual needs of the First Congregational Church, while his mom struggled to keep up with Dave and his two brothers and two sisters. His oldest brother, Howard, was big and strong and at least moderately retarded—way too much for Dave's mom to handle without occasional assistance from the police. Dave would lie on his bed, in the room he shared with both brothers, and stare up at the ceiling beams that had been made from whole trees, bark and all. He saw strange faces in the ridges and recesses of the tree bark. Demons. Devils. Staring back at him. He worried. And he wondered. He worried about his family, and he wondered why the doctors kept sending him back to this house to die.

Dave had felt like hell for about a year. Last season he'd been captain of the soccer team, the first kid picked for playground hoops, and getting wood on a Pony League fastball was as easy as smashing a badminton birdie. All this athletic stuff came so effortlessly, Dave didn't even think about it for fear that he'd somehow break the spell. But he *must* have been thinking about it, dammit, because this season everything was more difficult. The spell *was* broken. He couldn't get the bat around quick enough to catch up to the fastball. He'd started dribbling the basketball off his foot. He was a step too slow in soccer. His retarded brother was kicking his ass. At first his parents and coaches assumed that his sudden lack of coordination was a byproduct of puberty. His muscles were simply outpacing his brain's ability to control them. Dave wanted to believe this, so he practiced harder. He tried to concentrate, to will his body back to the well-tuned machine it had once been.

That's when he started falling down.

With no warning whatsoever. He'd be walking home from school and *bam*: face down on the pavement, shaking. It hurt, sure, but the worst thing was the embarrassment. He was twelve for Christ's sake, just carrying home a bag of groceries for his mom and the next thing he knew he was looking up at a bunch of people circled around him, yelling at each other to give him room to breathe, and his mom's groceries were scattered all over the sidewalk, green peppers and sweet onions rolling in the gutter.

The doctors couldn't figure Dave out. They thought Epilepsy. Muscular Dystrophy. Multiple Sclerosis. They didn't know what to think. They sent him to neurologists. They sent him to internists. They sent him to specialists who sent him home to worry and wonder.

One day Dave woke up and he couldn't see the faces in the ceiling beams anymore. He couldn't see anything. The world was hidden behind a sheet of manila paper. He felt his way downstairs and told his mom he was having trouble seeing.

"You probably just need glasses," Mrs. Cook said.

Even at twelve Dave knew this was bullshit, but his mom had to say something, so they both pretended that eyeglasses were the fix. The Cooks took Dave to see Dr. Paul Mitchell, an optometrist at Connecticut Children's in Hartford.

Maybe it was because he was young. Maybe it was because he was thorough. Whatever the case, Dr. Mitchell noticed something that every other doctor had missed—the brown and green rings that circled the periphery of Dave's corneas. Because Dave's eyes are blue, Dr. Mitchell could see these rings with just a pen light. But the doctor did more than notice the coppery lines encircling Dave's blue eyes; he gave them a name, Kayser-Fleisher rings. This was the first piece of tangible information the Cooks had received since Dave's symptoms began.

Dave remembers Dr. Mitchell then taking a solution of zinc or iron and holding a magnet to it, giving a charge to the ions. The doctor squeezed a few drops into Dave's eyes. Suddenly the doctor's office presented itself to Dave in all its sterile, fluorescent glory: the posters featuring various symptoms of corneal disease, the robotic-looking examination devices, the well-thumbed issues of *Popular Mechanics* and *Boys' Life*. Dave could see them all, and they were beautiful—but nowhere near as beautiful as the look of relief on his mom's face when Dr. Mitchell said, "I think I know what's wrong with your son."

***

Dave Cook is one of only a few thousand Americans with Wilson's disease, a disorder characterized by the body's inability to metabolize copper. Trace amounts of copper are in virtually everything we eat, and most of us get more of it than we need. We simply piss out the excess, just like we do with Vitamin C. But Dave's body holds onto copper the way penny-hoarders collect one-cent pieces. Since before he was born, his body has been retaining stores of the metal. In his liver. On his brain. In his eyes. By the time Dave visited Dr. Mitchell, not only had copper accumulated in the peripheral membranes of his corneas, but additional deposits had scarred organ tissue, short-circuited his central nervous system, and put him at the brink of liver and kidney failure.

The way Dave remembers it, enough copper had accumulated in his corneas to blind him. But in a series of e-mails, Dr. Mitchell tells me that although Kayser-Fleisher rings are a strong indicator of Wilson's disease, these rings never affect vision. Dave must have been blind with worry, blind with not knowing, blind with anger and frustration. Or maybe there is simply a blind spot in his memory, something lost in the journey from boy to man. Dr. Mitchell assures me there were no magic zinc or iron drops on that day in 1977. Dave must be thinking of the dilating drops used prior to the slit lamp examination. What is clear is this: To the Dave of today, Paul Mitchell remains a champion of the young and the sick. There is simply no telling Dave that the doctor did anything other than cure his blindness. End of story.

In Dr. Mitchell's office, now armed with a diagnosis, Mrs. Cook thought of the hundred-plus-year-old house that all the other doctors had sent Dave home to slowly die in. And she thought of the mineral-rich well water running through the house's copper pipes. And she wondered if she would ever forgive herself for poisoning her son.

The Cooks rushed Dave to Hartford Hospital, where the same neurosurgeon who had once told them, "I'm sorry Mr. and Mrs. Cook, there's nothing else I can do," now positioned himself as the resident expert on Wilson's disease. According to the Cooks, Dr. Neurosurgeon and his team thought *test case.* They thought *experimental treatments.* They thought *New England Journal of Medicine.* But they couldn't promise that Dave would live to see fifteen, let alone twenty-five or forty-two. The treatments were expensive and risky: Penicillamine—the medicine that would mine the copper from Dave's organs for excretion via his urine—can kill if the dosage isn't balanced just right against the amount of copper in the body. But left untreated, Wilson's is always fatal. Dave would die from copper poisoning.

Dave's dad didn't have health insurance, and trying to stretch a minister's salary to cover treatments for a rare disorder would have bankrupted the family. So the doctors steered the Cooks toward special programs and private donations to provide financial assistance. Dave was too young to appreciate the high-stakes negotiations involved in saving his life. He had no idea who was cutting the checks for all those doses of Penicillamine. Even today he's not exactly sure who paid for what. What Dave remembers now is not wanting to disappoint his mom by dying. He remembers how—despite having to keep a close eye on Howard and three other kids—she drove Dave back and forth across Connecticut, chasing down treatments that might cure him. These memories come back now when Dave notices his walk becoming more of a shuffle. They come back when he feels like he's about to fall. He remembers his mom's determination, and then he tightens his jaw and tries his damnedest to stay upright.

But he also remembers the afternoons he spent being pushed in a wheelchair down hospital halls. While other kids were horsing around on the soccer field and the ball diamond, he was staring out into lecture suites crowded with lab coats and stethoscopes. When the forty-two-year-old Dave imagines himself back in that wheelchair, the veins on his forehead pulse and the cords in his neck strain tight. On those afternoons, Dr. Neurosurgeon would refer to Dave as "The Patient," and every so often he would jab at Dave's liver and kidneys with a long pointer, drawing polite, golf-gallery applause. But after three or four laps around this lecture circuit, Dave got wise. He showed up to the next one with an empty Chock Full O'Nuts can in his lap. With his bowie knife he had cut an inch-long slot in the plastic lid. When Dr. Neurosurgeon asked about it, Dave said, "If you clowns want to wheel me around like a side-show freak, that's just fine. But it's gonna cost every one of you motherfuckers a dollar."

3. The Nine

On a sticky Columbus night in 1990, Dave Cook was manning the counter at Cloud Nine Pipes and Stuff. Friday dusk had given way to Friday dark, and all the tricked-out foreign jobs and rusted Caddies and Lincolns that pulled into this mini strip-mall had their headlights switched on. This meant that from his spot behind the cash register Dave could no longer see into the cars. He couldn't see who was coming and what they were bringing until they were already inside the store. Most customers only brought an itchy, strung-out desperation, but you just never knew who might be packing. So Dave assumed everybody was.

It smelled of incense and patchouli, but "The Nine" wasn't some quaint college town head shop that moved an occasional one-hitter between sales of Bob Marley and Che Guevara posters. This was no place for the mildly rebellious sorority girl who just bought her first copy of *Dark Side of the Moon*. Cloud Nine Pipes and Stuff was the big leagues. More pipes and less stuff. To wit: the display of glass stems sitting in an old test-tube holder on the counter by the cash register. Dave and his co-worker Pam and every other Nine employee would tell you that these glass stems were not—*were not*—crack pipes. They were *oil lamp filler tubes*.

Dave had been working at The Nine for six months. In the five years since he'd moved from Connecticut to Columbus, he'd landed a string of construction and auto-repair jobs, but due to layoffs, the seasonal nature of the work, or disagreements with supervisors, none of these gigs had lasted. He'd been eyeing the want ads for something steady when an ex-boss from the car wash introduced him to a guy who was looking for a trustworthy employee in an all-cash environment. With crooked employees and shoplifting customers, it was a tough racket running a smoke shop. And like all businesses in all sketchy neighborhoods, you learned to expect a little trouble. By now Dave knew The Nine was no worse off in the trouble department than Big Sonny's Pawn Shop or Yum-EE Donuts or the Sohio gas station. Still he was glad that *he* was on the clock tonight and not Pam.

Dave looked out toward Cleveland Avenue, four lanes running right up the gut of the Linden neighborhood. Linden in 1990 was an area of such desperation that the star attraction at the Pink Panther—the go-go bar that shared the parking lot with Cloud Nine—was a one-legged stripper. A buddy of Dave's was screwing this one-legged paramour of the Pink Panther, making himself a minor celebrity. Dave squinted and saw the Pink Panther's flashing neon reflected in the windshield of a car out in the lot. And from a billboard forty feet above the street, a smoothly handsome Billy Dee Williams and his beautiful caramel-skinned girlfriend assured Linden that Colt 45 malt liquor "works every time."

In the store windows, Dave could see his own reflection: Red Sox cap turned backward, Levi's spotted with mud and house paint, white muscle shirt gripping his finely chiseled torso. Much of his upper body had been given over to the tattoo needle, and he'd done almost all the work himself. An awfully high threshold of pain was required to hold that buzzing needle steady with his right hand as he dragged it across his left forearm and chest. But to Dave physical pain was only a nuisance, not so different from the mosquitoes that flew through Cloud Nine's open front door, made drunk by the fluorescent lighting. If some bad shit were to go down tonight, what could happen that would be any worse than what his own body had already dealt him? But just to be safe, he reached under the counter to feel for the 12 gauge, and he turned to double-check that the bush knife was close by.

Out in parking lot, the side door of a late-'70s Cutlass with new wire rims opened, and a forty-ounce bottle hit the blacktop and rolled down to the patch of weeds along the fence. Kids high on weed and warm beer bounced from car to car, talking varying degrees of shit. Dave knew they were mostly harmless. Young bucks from the neighborhood, working guys like him, just looking to tie on a buzz and a track down a piece of ass. They'd reached a sort of loose détente forged by necessity: their need of what Dave sold and Dave's need of a job. Until six weeks ago, Dave had never sweated these kids. He'd never sweated *any* of his customers.

But six weeks ago, Dave snapped.

It happened in the middle of the afternoon. Dave had been taking inventory in the stockroom when he heard Pam scream from out front. He dropped his clipboard and raced to the counter to see her standing in the door with tears in her eyes and the shotgun in her hands. The register drawer was open.

"Which way did he go?" Dave shouted. He ripped the gun from her and bolted down Cleveland Avenue. On the sidewalk in front of Picway Shoes, he tackled the would-be thief, and he marched the guy at gunpoint back to The Nine.

"I'm calling the cops," Pam said, as Dave prodded the thief through the store with the business end of the barrel.

"Fuck the cops. We're taking care of this asshole right here." Dave rammed the shotgun into the guy's kidneys. "Pam," he said over his shoulder. "Lock the door."

Five minutes earlier, Dave had been counting master cases of Joker rolling papers and Graffix water bongs in the stockroom. Now he shoved the thief into the stockroom and forced him to his hands and knees. Dave drove the gun barrel into the thin layer of neck skin shielding the guy's brain stem and pushed his head to the floor, face first. The shotgun tattooed a nickel-sized circle in the scruff of his neck. With his forehead butting the concrete floor, the thief's bowels let loose.

From the front of the store, Pam yelled, "Dave, I'm calling the damn cops!"

"No, Pam. Fuck no." Using the shotgun, Dave twisted the thief's head so the right side of his face was against the concrete. Dave jammed the gun into his sinus cavity.

Pam leaned through the stockroom door. "I'm *calling* the *police.*"

"Then you'd better tell 'em to hurry up, 'cause I'm about to paint the floor with this motherfucker."

The thief stiffened and garbled something unintelligible, pinned as he was between the shotgun and the floor. Dave raised the gun to the guy's temple to allow him to speak.

"Please, lady, please!" the thief screamed. "Call the police!"

***

On this Friday night, six weeks after that robbery attempt, Dave was still sporting a yellow bruise under his cheekbone from where the cops had bashed him with nightsticks as they wrestled the shotgun from him. He still tasted the blood seeping through his teeth and dripping down the back of his throat. He still felt a hot flash of adrenaline every time somebody he didn't recognize walked into The Nine.

Just then one of Dave's regular oil lamp filler tube customers came shaking through the door. Flag-pole thin with a runny nose, he was about thirty-five and wearing an old army parka with fur around the hood, even though it was eighty degrees easy.

"Hey, man. What can I get for you?" Dave asked, remembering the last time this dude was in here. He'd been so hard-up looking, Dave went ahead and palmed him a free filler tube. With crackheads, you want them in and out. Quick. That's why the test tube holder was right next to the register. Crackheads are bad for business. They're shifty and desperate and lately they made the salivary glands in Dave's cheeks secrete that bloody metallic taste. Crackheads made Dave's bruised cheek and jaw itch.

"I'm just checkin' out the papers, man," the guy said, nodding at rolling papers up on the shelf behind the register.

Dave said, "Okay, whatever," even as he was thinking, *Who the hell window shops for papers?* "Let me know when you need something."

"You got change for the bus?"

"No problem, dude." Dave hit the "No Sale" button on the side of the register, took the guy's crumpled single off the glass countertop, and handed him a stack of quarters. He pushed the drawer shut. "What else?" *In and out.*

"How much you say them papers were?"

"A dollar seventy-five. You want 'em?"

"Naw. I'm straight." The guy wiped his nose on the sleeve of his parka.

"Well, you gotta buy something. You can't—" And the phone started ringing.

Dave hated turning his back on a crackhead, so he tried to keep one eye on the dude as he turned to answer the phone, which was up on the shelf next to the rolling papers. "Cloud Nine. Hello."

"Yeah," said the caller. "Uh, how much are your, uh, rolling papers—"

Still feeling the nervous residue from the robbery six weeks ago, Dave's mind was churning: *Change for the bus. No Sale. Rolling papers. Back on the shelf. By the phone. Phone ringing. How much you say them papers were? Who calls about rolling papers? This is too fucking weird.* He grabbed hold of the eighteen-inch bush knife he'd started keeping behind the counter.

And right then, from behind, Dave heard the *tink-tink* of glass filler tubes being jostled in their holder. He tightened his grip on the knife handle and spun back toward the cash register. The crackhead jerked his hand away from the "No Sale" button that would have opened the cash drawer.

The guy almost got his hand away clean. Almost. But the knife came down hard, cracking the countertop and sending forty-odd glass stems toppling off the counter onto the floor. The crackhead raised his right hand to his face and screamed at the bloody stump that used to be his pinkie finger.

A half-hour later Dave was wiping up blood with Formula 409 and paper towels. *Fuck this*, he thought. *$6.25 an hour is nowhere near enough money for me to have to put up with this shit.*

As Dave pressed strips of duct tape to the spider webbed cracks in the countertop, one of the parking lot b-boys, a smallish kid of about twenty, walked through the front door.

"What's up," Dave said, trying to tune out the buzzing adrenaline rattling around in his skull, making the tips of his ears hot.

"Lemme get two of them blunts right there," the kid said, "and— what the fuck is that?" He was looking at the mass of graying meat and bone that Dave had nailed to the wall next to the register. "Is that a knuckle? Is that a damn *fingernail*?"

"What?" said Dave, following the kid's horrified stare, letting all the rage come back, not even bothering to fight it. "This here? This piece of shit, right fucking here?"

"Yeah, wha—"

"You fucking know what this is?"

"Naw, man. I gotta be going—"

"This," Dave said, "is the pinkie finger of the last motherfucker that tried to rob me. I'm starting a collection." He reached for the bush knife. "You wanna be next?"

4. War Is Not the Answer

"I can't talk about this shit anymore," Dave says, shooting a suspect glance at the tape recorder that has been rolling for more than an hour.

He says nothing for what feels like five minutes. He just swivels his head back and forth, his eyes squinting to thin slits, his face two shades whiter. I spend the silent minutes feeling like an asshole. My prodding has brought these memories to the surface, and I wonder if I'm any different from that neurosurgeon back in Connecticut, dragging Dave through his own story because it suits my needs— because I think his story is important.

Dave doesn't think of himself as important. Because if he *is*, then he has to wonder if it's the illness that makes him so. He won't give Wilson's disease that kind of respect.

He rises from the Papasan and starts doing laps around the bedroom. "There was a lot of hate in my body back then," he finally says.

I think about hitting stop on the recorder. But I don't.

"And I'm not proud of some of the shit I've done to people." He takes a charred Bic from the chest pocket of his overalls and lights what must be his millionth Marlboro of the night. "But the thing is, you give me a paycheck, and I'll fucking work for it. Part of my job at The Nine was to protect the cash? I'm gonna protect the goddamn cash."

Dave still works at the smoke shop, but now, in addition to his usual shifts behind the register, he's also a bodyman and mechanic for the Cloud Nine auto-racing team. He shrinks dents and drops radiators for a measly eight bucks an hour while his boss makes enough money selling oil lamp filler tubes to maintain a fleet of racecars.

He sits back down and starts rubbing his temples, and I brace for another long silence. Instead, Dave starts laughing. "But these days?" he says, smoke leaking from between his incisors. "These days I'd say, 'You want the cash register, motherfucker? You can have it. I'll even carry it out to your car for you.'"

***

At forty-two Dave Cook worries that he's getting soft. Or maybe he's getting smart. He's not sure. He just knows he doesn't feel the same hatred he used to. The rage that has coursed through his veins for so long, giving him the strength to fight a rare disease and enemies real and imagined, has subsided. And this worries him. He wonders if Wilson's has finally worn him down for good. Or maybe it's the medicine that's stripping him of his edge. For whatever reason, he's scared. He feels so *passive* these days. For as long as he can remember, he's never run from a fight. He's spent his whole life looking for one.

"But I can't get pissed off enough anymore, you know?" he says. "You get to that point where you gotta decide: Do I want to fight or do I want to crumble? And lately I'm thinking, 'Fuck it, man. Crumble.'" He turns his head to the side and bites down, his jaw hard as a walnut. "And every day I see that goddamn sticker on your mom's car, and she's right, man. War is not the answer."

After fifteen years of doing odd jobs for my family and friends, Dave recently caved and let my mom give him her old car as payment. Now a Suzuki Sidekick with a *War Is Not the Answer* bumper sticker sits in his driveway. Every morning Dave climbs into the Suzuki and drives forty miles up to Mt. Gilead, where he puts the Dave Cook Hot Tweak on his boss's racecar engines. Dave sets the gaps in the plugs to his personal specs, so that when the current ignites the mix of fuel and oxygen that drives the pistons, Team Cloud Nine might shave a second or two off their next trip around the 1/3-mile track at Columbus Motor Speedway.

"Now, up in Mt. goddamn Gilead, boy, they love them some God, guns, and G. W. fucking Bush. And you better believe they drive American cars. Then there's me tooling around in that little Suzuki with goddamn *War Is Not the Answer* on the back. Shit, I might as well paint a giant rainbow on the motherfucker and start drinking bottled water and singing show tunes, you know what I mean?" Dave's laughing again. "And I just know, *I just fucking know*, I'm gonna be stopped at a red light and some asshole is gonna roll up and say something. And then I'm gonna have to fight some redneck Marine." He angles his forearms across his thighs and leans forward. "Thing is," he says, "until about six months ago, I'd a never sweated it. If anybody ever came up on me, well, there are ways to take people out. But now I ain't so sure."

Until about six months ago, I'd a never sweated it.

Six months ago Dave shelled out a thousand dollars and took the deed on the house. For a man who has struggled for ownership of even something as fundamental as his own body, this was a rare win. Dave has fought the workings of his biology for a long time, and he'll surely take more ass-kickings in years to come. But in Cook Acres he possesses something he can control. He doesn't have to fight. If the septic system breaks, he just fixes it. He's got the tools and the know-how and a crew of buddies for when he needs extra muscle. He can crack open the house's chest and manipulate its internal organs—working the same magic he's performed so many times under a hood. On this patch of land, Dave Cook doesn't wait for a diagnosis from anybody.

***

Cole barks to be let in. He leaves a trail of muddy paw prints on the bedroom floor as he runs up to Dave and licks his face. Dave breaks into a smile that deepens the wrinkles around his eyes. "But you know that sticker on my car? I *did* get a comment." He wipes away the dog spit with the sleeve of his sweatshirt. "I was sitting in the parking lot at Kroger's, and this dude starts knocking on my window. I roll it down and get ready for whatever wiseass comment, and you know what he says? He says, 'Right on, brother. War is *not* the answer.' And I looked down at his tie-dye shirt and his sandals and socks, and I had to feel for the dude, man. I had to *feel* for him. Because I know he gets his ass kicked everywhere he goes."

Walking toward the window that will one day throw light on his kitchen, Dave shakes his head and laughs. "'Right on, brother. War is *not* the answer.' Can you believe that shit?"

He opens a new bag of Pedigree Complete Nutrition dog food and pours Cole a bowlful of fresh water from a plastic jug. "You know what I want now?"

I look up to the ceiling support beams. In four-inch letters—drawn with a thick, red marker and positioned directly over his bed—he has written: *GET UP YOU PUSSY! (we will not surrender to pain)*.

Dave slides his sleeves up his tattooed forearms. An Indian chief. A tomahawk. A streak of flames. He's leaning against the plywood walls of his house. "You know what I *really* want?" he says. "All I want is to wake up one morning and make a fresh pot of coffee in my new kitchen and feel the sun coming in the windows. Then I'm gonna go out on my back deck, under all these trees, and I'm gonna sip that coffee, and I'm gonna smoke a cigarette, and I'm just gonna stand there. I'm gonna stand there and enjoy it without a fucking care in the world. Ain't gonna worry about shit."

—*2008*

Partisans

I'm sitting on an overstuffed couch in the Mexican home of a big Alabaman named Chuck, drinking Dos Equis and watching college football via pirated satellite. Kate is leaning against the kitchen counter, knitting a wool cap, smiling politely at Chuck's friend, a Texan who calls himself The Mayor. His Honor—wearing a Hawaiian shirt and flip-flops, his hair gringo-in-Mexico long—could be Matthew McConaughey's less handsome, less famous older brother. From my spot on the couch, it sounds like he's giving Kate the full and complete accounting of how fan-damn-tastic his life down here in the Yucatán is, but I can't say for sure because I'm staring at the TV, a fat-backed, low-def model on which the Ohio State Buckeyes are about to take the field against the Texas Longhorns. Kate and I are from Columbus, and we're both in grad school at OSU, so this is a must-see game for us—for me, I should say. Kate thinks football is boring and overvalued, hence the knitting needles and the self-banishment to the kitchen with The Mayor, who would apparently rather chat up a pretty Brit Lit scholar than watch the most anticipated contest of the 2005 season. Number 4 Ohio State versus Number 2 Texas. The first-ever meeting of these two powerhouse programs. The Horseshoe all lit up for the prime-time slot on ABC. Yep, I'm talking about a football game. An important one. The sole reason Kate and I are here on the dirt-road-and-roaming-dog outskirts of Valladolid, Mexico, with two men we don't know.

In a week and a half, we'll be back on campus for the start of fall quarter, but right now Kate and I are still putting a celebratory cap on the summer, thanks to the credit card miles we exchanged for flights to Cancún. After a few beach days on Isla Mujeres, we hopped a bus and rode two hours inland to Valladolid, which, as we'd read in *Lonely Planet*, is a convenient base for a visit to the ancient city of Chichén Itzá. We spent most of yesterday on the grounds of that UNESCO World Heritage Site, and the Temple of Kukulkan and the Wall of Skulls were just as spectacular as advertised. Once we got back to the hotel, however, with *Mayan Ruins* now crossed off the list of sights to see, my priority became tracking down a place to watch the OSU/Texas game.

So I told Kate we needed to do some reconnaissance work that night. Find out who, if anyone, in this part of Mexico had the proper satellite configuration to beam down some good ol' NCAA football the next day. I knew that if we'd still been near Cancún, we'd have been able to find the game in any number of tourist bars, but out here in the provinces there weren't any tourist bars. Hopefully, though, with the University of Texas—the flagship school in a state that was once *part* of Mexico—being half the equation, we'd get lucky.

The desk clerk at our hotel suggested we ask at a bar down the street, across from Parque Francisco Cantón, the town square. The place was full of locals, everybody but us speaking Spanish, and the steak tampiqueña was delicious. The tequila, equally so. But the presence of just one TV mounted in the corner—tuned on a Friday night to a Latin American version of the Home Shopping Network—suggested that this establishment wasn't exactly College Football HQ.

By this point, I had resigned myself to missing the game, and I was suddenly okay with it. Kate and I were full of food and booze and mystic Mayan history. We were laughing and having a great time. We were *living*, man. Grad students loose in the world, doing stuff. Not sitting in front of the tube, watching other people do stuff.

Then, from out of the barroom white noise, I heard somebody say "Texas." Not Tejas, but *Texas*. In pure American. I looked over, and there was a gringo in a Hawaiian shirt and flip-flops, sitting at a table with a group of well-dressed Mexicans.

"Hang on a second," I said to Kate, and I scooted my chair back. Of the two of us, she was the one more likely to strike up a bar conversation with a stranger, but I was buzzed enough, and the stakes of the football game were high enough, that I walked right up to the guy's table and asked him if he was a Longhorns fan.

He shot me a confused look.

"Sorry," I said. "I thought I heard you say something about Texas."

"Best damn state there is," he said, raising his beer bottle. Within a minute I had the quick bio. Texas native, now living in Valladolid. Engineer with an American utility company that was building a power plant nearby. I asked him how he liked it here, and he clapped his hands together and said, "Love it."

"Of course, he loves it," one of the Mexican guys said in barely accented English. "He runs this town."

"Runs this town" sounded like sarcasm—but not exactly. More like a nebulous coordinate between irony and truth. Either way, the gringo dismissed it with a wave and then extended his hand to me. "They call me The Mayor."

If college football was to be had in this part of the Yucatán, it seemed like the local dignitary here would know, so I asked him if there was a sports bar anywhere close.

He laughed. "Nothing like that," he said. "But hang tight for a minute." He looked over at Kate and toasted his beer toward her. She lifted her glass in return. He pulled his cell phone from his shorts. "Let me make a few calls."

I went back to our table, and The Mayor aimed for the front door, dialing as he walked. Kate asked what had happened. "I'm not sure," I said. I turned toward the entrance. "But that guy seems to be lobbying for us."

A few minutes later, he tapped me on the shoulder. He was holding his cell to his ear, and he motioned for me to follow him outside. Once on the sidewalk, he reached toward me with the phone and said, "Say hi to Chuck." Right then, two girls walked by. They were wearing loose tops and tight jeans, and they were young. Way too young. We were invisible to them. They were highly visible to us. "Unh-unh-unh," The Mayor said, shaking his head. He looked them up and down, and after they passed, he kept looking. "I do love this place."

"Hello?" I said into the phone. "Chuck?"

With a mid-Southern accent, he was obviously from the States. He told me he'd be watching football all day tomorrow. At his house. And as long as I didn't mind that his first priority was the Alabama game, which was scheduled to kick off just fifteen minutes before OSU/Texas, he'd be happy to invite us over. We'd just have to flip back and forth between channels. "Where you staying?" he asked. "I'll come and pick you up. Look for a big guy in a little car."

Accepting a ride from a man I knew only by phone, a man whose single character reference came courtesy of the lecherous Mayor, sounded sketchy, but Kate and I were seasoned-enough travelers—in our fifteen years together we'd been to Turkey and Venezuela, and we'd once spent three months driving a van through Mexico—to know that oftentimes the best and most memorable experiences of a trip are those that seem potentially dangerous in the moment. The only sure way to avoid sketchiness is to sequester yourself within the walls of a swank resort, but what's the point of traveling if you never leave the lounge chair?

So I gave him the name of our hotel, thanked him, and said we'd see him tomorrow. And sure enough, earlier this evening, Chuck appeared at the curb, all six-foot-something, upper-two-hundred pounds of him, leaning into the passenger side of a Ford Fiesta that was a color I'd call maroon but a 'Bama fan would definitely call crimson. The car was the same shade of red as his UA t-shirt, which he wore along with jeans and arch-friendly white sneakers.

I waved to let him know that Kate and I were the couple he was looking for, but he already knew. The three of us were the only light-skinned people around. As we walked toward Chuck and his car, I wondered what the scene looked like to the Mexican cabbies and cart-vendors that were watching us. Like a gringo family reunion, maybe. Big older brother reunites with little bro and his wife. My guess was that to the Valladolid locals, Chuck and I didn't look all that different. His skin was as pale as mine. He was as bald as I am. But he had me by six inches and 125 pounds. If you could stick an air valve in my belly button and blow me up with helium, the result would be something Chuck-like.

"You ready?" he said. He opened the car door for us, and we climbed in.

***

A ten-minute drive on roads that ran from colonial cobblestone to potholed asphalt to dirt, and now we're here are at Chuck's place, a small ranch that's utterly nonthreatening in its bachelor-pad blandness. No hint of Mexico's ubiquitous bright colors. Everything is beige-on-beige. Beige carpet and wall paint, beige countertops and cabinets. No knickknacks. Nada hanging on the walls. Nothing to suggest that we're sitting in the Yucatán as opposed to a $150-per-week extended-stay off I-70 in Kansas City. Mexico seems only to exist outside, in the neighborhood, where chickens are clucking and laundry is drying on split-rail-and-wire fences. Here on the inside, we're not in Mexico; we're in the Chuck Republic, and that's fine with me. I only came here to watch football.

And on the gridiron, the night is off to a disappointing start for Chuck, me, and our teams. At the end of the first quarter, Texas is shutting out Ohio State 10-0. Chuck's Crimson Tide are down four to Southern Mississippi. Both games are still in the early stages, and the Dos Equis is helping to keep our optimism up, but the next round of four beers I grab from the fridge leaves us with only a few bottles. Kate and I are terrible guests. The big man was thoughtful enough to invite two complete strangers into his house, and we didn't even have the courtesy to bring booze. Somewhere Emily Post is looking down with a *tsk-tsk*. To be fair, on the way here, I asked Chuck to stop at a store so I could buy beer, but the 'Bama game was about to start, and he didn't want to risk missing kickoff. He thought he had enough Dos Equis at home to last until halftime. We could make a run to the store then. But now, even with the six-pack The Mayor contributed when he showed up, rations are running low.

Chuck flips to his game for the start of the second quarter, and Alabama immediately goes three and out. They're forced to punt. "Goddammit," he says, hammering his hand into the armrest of his La-Z-Boy.

As a sports fan, I empathize with Chuck. The Tide should be crushing the Golden Eagles. I don't feel any special allegiance to Alabama; in fact, were I watching this game anywhere else, I'd be cheering against them, rooting for the underdogs from Hattiesburg, a team that had been forced to cancel the opening game of their season because of Hurricane Katrina, which struck twelve days ago. But as a guest in a 'Bama fan's house, a guest who showed up empty-handed, rooting for the home team seems like what Emily Post would do. "The Tide's got too much talent for these suckers to hang with 'em much longer," I say, hoping to put my host at ease.

Seven plays later, Southern Miss scores to take a 21-10 lead. Chuck smacks his left palm with his right fist loud enough to get the attention of Kate and The Mayor, who look in on us from the kitchen. Chuck clicks over to the OSU game and then grunts up out of the recliner and heads for the fridge. A field goal has put the Buckeyes on the scoreboard, so I'm feeling a little sunnier, and the cold beer and channel switch have combined to calm Chuck down a notch. As Texas begins their possession, he starts telling me about his job here in Valladolid. He's a manager for a company that makes blue jeans—some brands I've heard of, some not. He pinches the thigh fabric on the pants he's wearing. "We made these," he says.

He uses the words *plant* and *factory*, but I'm thinking *maquiladora*. And I'm imagining Chuck, the big bossman, stalking the floor, trying to get his employees' fingers to fly ever faster through their machines.

"These Mexicans, boy," Chuck says, "they're some hard-ass workers."

"I bet," I say, swiveling my head between him and the TV but still thinking about a phalanx of seamstresses, bent to their industrial Singers, risking their digits for who knows how many pesos per hour.

"*Hard*-ass workers." He swigs his beer. "Not like the blacks back home. Believe me."

Oh, no. Here we go. I brace myself for his next sentence, which will undoubtedly be *"I'm not a racist, but…"* The line I've heard a hundred times—just us, brother, white man to white man—back in Ohio and all over America. I say nothing, hating Chuck a little already. But he doesn't continue, doesn't move that particular ball forward. And soon I'm clapping because the Buckeyes have forced the Longhorns to punt, and over the next few minutes, as OSU marches into Texas territory, the conversation stays on the relatively safe ground of sports. I can almost forget what Chuck said and almost forgive him for saying it.

Then, on third and long, Buckeye quarterback Troy Smith hits Santonio Holmes on a 36-yard touchdown strike that has me bouncing out of the couch. From the kitchen, Kate raises a knitting needle in support. Even Chuck lets out a cheer. The score is tied 10-10, and the TV broadcast goes to a close-up of Holmes on the sideline, helmet off, flashing a perfect post-touchdown smile, his hair twisted into chin-length dreads.

"Look at that," Chuck says. "That boy's still got some ol' cotton-patch nigger in him."

My head turns toward the La-Z-Boy in stunned reflex. I must be wearing a facial expression that reveals my horror, but even if I am, Chuck doesn't notice. He's staring at Holmes on the screen in much the same way The Mayor looked at those young girls last night. Sexualized—but also scientific. Like he's constructing a taxonomy.

I know what I should do. I should drop my bottle to the coffee table, stand up, and say, "Thanks so much for your hospitality, Chuck, but we've gotta be going. Can you please take us home?" But I don't do that. I'm too big a coward to do that. Instead, I say nothing. I do nothing—except look over at Kate to make sure she didn't hear Chuck's violent uncoiling of the n-word, because if she had heard it, she'd be packing up her yarn right now.

I spend the next few minutes furious with Chuck and with myself. I'm mad at Chuck for hauling out that hateful word, sure, but also for being such a cliché. Why'd you have to be from Alabama of all places? Why do you have to fit so neatly into a stereotype I'm fighting not to harbor? The last thing I want to be is one of those hypocritical urban white Northerners who is bigoted against rural white Southerners. The world is complicated, Chuck. Not easily boxed and taxonomized. Damn you for making it so easy for me to be intellectually lazy, for making it so easy for me to dismiss you.

But again, as pissed as I am at Chuck, I'm angrier with myself. I know I can justify my having said and done nothing. I've got a slew of excuses: I'm a guest in his house. He could easily kick my ass. He could refuse to drive Kate and me home, leaving us stranded out here on the dirt roads, with the chickens and dirty laundry. He might have a pistol hidden under his seat cushion. Besides, Chuck and I are not friends, and I'm not going to change his mind about anything. Game night at Casa del Chuck is not the place for a debate on racial acceptance. Even so, the legitimacy of my excuses doesn't make me feel any better about my shameful silence.

And more shameful still: I really want to watch this game. I mean, come on. The Bucks just tied it up. If Kate and I cut and run now, the racial terrorists win.

So I tell myself that I'll extract my revenge against Chuck by colonizing his house and exploiting his natural resources (meaning the bootleg satellite dish and the beer, what's left of it). And, on the inside anyway, I'll cheer so hard for the Golden Eagles to upset Alabama that the University of Southern Mississippi will award me an Honorary Doctorate in Partisanship. Southern Miss to the top! Chuck and the Crimson Tide must go to bed tonight in defeat.

***

Chuck switches the TV back to 'Bama, and for a while, everything is working out perfectly for Southern Mississippi fans like me. Alabama's kicker misses a 41-yard field goal, and Chuck again tenderizes the armrest. On their next possession, the Tide goes three and out, and Chuck looks ready to pop an aneurysm. With just over three minutes until halftime, UA is backed up at their own 28-yard line, still down 21-10. The Buckeyes, meanwhile, have kicked two field goals to take a 16-10 lead over the Longhorns. Six more points for the good guys.

For Chuck, it keeps getting worse. Alabama is penalized for a false start. Then for holding. Then for an illegal block. When the broadcast cuts to the instant replay of this last infraction, Chuck shakes his head at the guilty 'Bama player and spits out, "Goddamn nigger."

I'm doubly shocked. First of all, he's now using that word against a kid who's wearing a jersey that's the same color as his own t-shirt.

These are his guys, his team, and even they aren't immune from his venom. Secondly, most of the racists I know are smart enough—or maybe I should say *shrewd* enough—not to voice their prejudicial thoughts in polite company. So what does it mean that Chuck is comfortable using the n-word in front of me? By not protesting against his earlier cotton-patch remark, did I give him reason to think I agree with him? Does he think I'm *like* him? Does my silence amount to tacit permission for him to keep talking that garbage, and, if so, then *am* I in fact like him?

On the inside, I'm seething. I wish for a spring in the La-Z-Boy seat to break loose under Chuck's weight and bite him in the ass. I wish for a meteorite to come crashing through the roof and score a direct hit on Chuck, leaving me free to watch the Buckeye game in the warmth of his smoldering carcass. When neither of those happens, I take comfort in the fact that Chuck's team is losing by eleven at home to a directional school from lowly Conference USA.

With twenty-nine seconds until halftime, 'Bama is stuck with a fourth-and-13 from the USM 43 yard line. Quarterback Brodie Croyle takes the shotgun snap and heaves a desperation pass to receiver Tyrone Prothro, who is being well covered by a Southern Miss defender. Despite having a man literally in his face, Prothro grabs the ball out of the air and traps it against the back of the player that's covering him. Joined front-to-front—with Prothro's arms wrapped around the defender, pinning the football to the back of that guy's shoulder pads—the two players roly-poly into the end zone, and somehow Prothro maintains control of the ball throughout the somersault. He stands up, holding the ball in the air as if to say, *See this here? I caught this thing.* The officials initially signal incomplete, but after a short conference, the refs agree that it was a legal catch.

Chuck catapults out of the recliner and lets loose a whoop. "Hell yeah, son," he says to the image of Prothro on the television, "that's how you do it!"

Kate and The Mayor come into the living room for a look at the replay, and on the TV, the broadcast team dissects the grab from all angles. Announcer Mark Jones calls it the catch of the year in college football, even though the season is only two weeks old. Color analyst Chris Spielman calls it maybe the best catch he's ever seen.

Chuck leans toward me for a high-five. I give him one. "Fuckin' A," he says. "Goddamn amazing."

It is an amazing catch, definitely one of the best I've ever seen. But I'm just as amazed at how easily Chuck can pivot from disparaging one black 'Bama player to praising another. Absolute hatred in one instant; unadulterated delight in the next.

The Buckeye Football schedule I keep in my wallet tells me that tonight is September 10th, so back home a textile mill's worth of American flags are being hung. As Chuck watches replay after replay, I'm wondering: How do we decide to whom and what we pledge allegiance? Whose fight song do we sing? Whose jersey do we wear? Are these borders hard and fast? Or are they openings, frontiers, *fronteras*. If a Mexican guy—maybe a disgruntled worker from the blue jeans factory—were to kick down the door right now and start to threaten Chuck, which of the two men would I line up alongside? Would I stand with the guy who looks like me, who's from where I'm from, who was nice enough to welcome us into his house? Or would I stand with the pissed-off Mexican? *Damn straight, amigo. I hate this bastard, too. Let's get him.* When it's time to choose sides, what matters more, proximity or principles?

The officials place the ball on the 1-yard line, and on the following play Alabama scores a touchdown to cut the deficit to 21-17 heading into halftime. Chuck is smiling big and goofy like a kindergartner on Christmas, and on his face I can see what he must have looked like thirty years and two-hundred pounds ago, when he was a kid growing up in Alabama, trying to figure out where he stood and who he stood with. He offers me the last beer out of the fridge, then we flip to the Buckeye game in time to see the Longhorns drill a field goal that trims Ohio State's lead to 16-13 at the break. The Buckeyes and Golden Eagles are both still winning, but barely.

***

When The Mayor volunteers to make the beer run, I hand him a two hundred-peso note. "We got this," I say.

He slides the bill into his front pocket. "Who's going with me?"

He's ostensibly asking all of us, but he's looking at Kate. I can tell she's weighing the pros and cons. Going means adventure, local color. Staying means more meaningless football.

Chuck levers open the footrest on the recliner. "Second half's about to start," he says, angling the chair toward forty-five degrees, clearly intent on staying put.

I look at my watch. No way we'll be back in time for the start of the third quarter of the Buckeye game.

The Mayor raises his brow at Kate. "Any takers?"

"Okay," she says. "I'll go." She looks at me and raises her shoulders as if to say, *Dicey, I know. But in for a dime, in for a dollar.*

Kate doesn't know how dicey. She didn't see the look The Mayor gave those girls on the sidewalk, and I didn't tell her because I didn't want her to nix our one opportunity to watch the game. I'm certain she hasn't heard Chuck throw around the n-word.

"You sure you don't want company, honey?" I say.

"I *am* the company," she says, packing her needles and wool into a market bag and grabbing her purse.

"All right!" The Mayor gives a double thumbs up. "On the way we can stop by the house I was telling you about," he says to Kate. "The one I'm fixing up."

His *house*? I'm trying to send her a look that says *I know you're a strong woman, but I don't think leaving with this guy is a good idea.* And yet, somewhere deep in the meekest corner of myself, I'm hoping she'll insist that I don't come, that I stay, which means I'll be able to sit here and continue watching football with a man I dislike. And even as this negotiation is happening, I realize that of all the mistakes I've made tonight, this is the one I'll regret the most. Because if I know nothing else, I know that my true loyalty should be to Kate—the partner I voluntarily chose and who in return chose me. This is the team that matters. The two of us. United by proximity and principle, pledges and vows. "You *sure*, Kate?" I say.

"Yeah," she says. "I got it. You stay and enjoy your football." She gives me a kiss and then walks to the door and stands next to The Mayor. "See you in a bit." They take off together.

The 'Bama game is back on the TV. Chuck, still buoyed by the Prothro catch at the end of the first half, is sitting on the edge of his seat, saying, "Come on, boys. Stick it to 'em."

I'm hoping like hell that the Golden Eagles can hang on to their lead, that the scales of football justice can punish Chuck in ways that I'm unable to. But that isn't what happens. I don't know it yet, but Alabama will win tonight, and Ohio State will lose. And later, when we're back at the hotel, Kate will tell me that when The Mayor took her on the tour of his house, she was holding her knitting needles at the ready. If he tried to lay a hand on her, she was prepared to go for the throat. Trach-city, Your Honor.

But right now, as Alabama kicks off to Southern Miss to start the second half, I'm still berating myself for my stupidity. I've just handed The Mayor my wife—and, as a kicker, 200 pesos of seed money. I had the chance to pick sides, and I chose Chuck and football. For the whole long hour Kate is gone, I keep thinking that if the fictitious worker from the blue jeans factory were to boot down the door now, irate and itching to fight, here's what he'd see: Two bald gringos. Sitting next to each other, staring at the action. A couple of all-American benchwarmers.

—*2016*

Tricoter

We'd looked at things. We'd tried new drinks. But this morning, Kate and I didn't feel up to mingling with the clear-eyed, spring-stepping window shoppers of the Rue des Abbesses. We had no interest in seeing our hangovers reflected back at us in the pink faces of the Montmartre's *boulangerie* and *pâtisserie* patrons, they of the ever-fashionable Burberry plaid. So we lowered our eyes to the sidewalk and followed the pressure in our frontal lobes to the dimly lit, wood paneled Café Le Baroudeur—the kind of place where you can order a beer before noon and not feel guilty. Kate and I are perched on stools at the first table by the window. On the other side of the glass, the Place des Abbesses is dolled-up with *décorations de Noël*. It's eight days until Christmas, and a blue sky hangs over Paris for the first time since we arrived here a week ago. But the Café Le Baroudeur is smoky as a bowling alley on league night. Above our table, a sliver of sunlight plays tricks with the floating ash. Kate is rummaging through her bag, looking for her knitting needles. I'm writing in my journal. We're not speaking presently. Well, Kate's not anyway.

"You want coffee?" I say, running my tongue across the sweaters of my teeth.

Kate's attention is focused on the scarf she's knitting my dad for Christmas. "Whatever," she says.

I motion toward the bartender, "Deux cafés-au-lait, s'il vous plaît."

He brings the coffees on a serving tray. Two cups, two saucers, and a few Euro-long sugar packets with *Lavazza* printed on the side. I turn one of these packets end over end. The granules flow down and then down again: from L to A and A to L and back. Kate's hands are a tangle of silver needles and alpaca wool. I watch her fingers go through their calisthenics. *Pull yarn–Wrap around–Push through–Yank off. Purl stitch. Knit stitch. Purl stitch.*

"What's wrong?" I say, tearing open the sugar and pouring it over my coffee.

Kate doesn't look up from her knitting. "Nothing." *Pull yarn.*

"Do you want to—"

"I don't want to talk. I'm fine." *Wrap around.*

"Look. I'm sorry I dragged you across half of Paris last night. I had no idea the Metro quit running—"

"It's not that." *Push through. Yank off.*

I drop my palms to the table, and my wedding ring makes a popping sound on the wood. "What is it then?"

"Nothing." *Purl stitch. Knit stitch. Purl stitch.*

***

Open on the table before me is an unlined Moleskine, the notebook allegedly used by the turn-of-the-century Parisian avant-garde. I know it's ridiculous to think I can channel the intellectual magic of the Lost Generation simply by heading to Barnes and Noble and buying the journal with proper literary bloodlines. And yet, here I am: an Ohioan in Paris who likes to think of himself as the type Hemingway, Gertrude Stein, and Sherwood Anderson would have saved a seat for at Les Deux Magots.

I'm eighty-five years late for my swig at the Absinthe bottle. The crumbs of that movable feast have long been swept up. But across

the Seine, the Place St. Germain des Prés—a boutique-lined inter-
section that patrons of Les Deux Magots gaze upon from behind
their 6.00 € *chocolat chauds*—continues to cash-in on its artistic
and intellectual past. Tourists from around the world descend on
that hallowed spot in La Rive Gauche hoping to get a noseful of the
air expelled by Sartre, de Beauvior, and Picasso, luminaries who if
they were alive today would surely take one sideways glance at Les
Deux Magots' distinctly un-bohemian clientele and decide to walk
on by. Hemingway would never stand shoulder to shoulder at the
bar with the tour-bus set, forced to share an ashtray with Mitch and
Helen Baughman of the Bloomfield Hills Baughmans—Mitch, a
mid-level purchasing executive at Ford, and Helen, a retired middle
school teacher with snowmen and candy canes appliquéd to her
sweater. It's the same at all the old haunts. Le Café de Flore? The
Baughmans have been there. Harry's Bar? The Baughmans have
done that. The American Bar at La Closerie des Lilas? The Baughmans have already FedEx'd the souvenir t-shirt home to their son
Trevor, a sophomore at Michigan State. *Once they take it away,
Papa,* I think, hunched over my journal, *you never get it back.*

***

At the Café Le Baroudeur's mahogany bar, an old-timer *clink-
clanks* a demitasse cup against its saucer to signal to the bartender
that he's ready for another espresso. Except for a pencil-thin moustache, his face is three days unshaven and lined with stubble the
color of gourmet pepper: a patchy dash of reds, blacks, and grays. Is
he a rough forty or a well-preserved sixty? He's wearing a long-out-
of-fashion double-breasted suit and dirty Nikes, but he has acces-
sorized this outfit with such strange, dandified flourishes that he
maintains an air of superiority, like he's the last-standing sophisti-
cate in the 18th Arrondissement. His dapper felt hat is cocked
just-so, the brim turned down in front and up in back to reveal the

scruff of an untrimmed neck. The tailored but wrinkled flannel suit hanging on his wiry frame speaks of an impoverished elegance, of a history of fuck-ups so glorious as not to be believed by mere civilians.

This Bum-Dandy of the Rue des Abbesses is standing at the bar, but he's not leaning on it. He won't stay still long enough to leave his weight on any singular point. His movements are multi-hinged, like a puppet's or a break-dancer's—herky-jerky rather than fluid, a series of snaps and pops and petit mal seizures. And yet this is somehow graceful, not in the calculated manner of a drunk feigning sobriety, but more like a colt shaking off the sleep of the womb. His limbs seem to unfold in all directions at once. For the Bum-Dandy, a routine gesture like digging in his pocket for change is a dance that starts at his running shoes and shivers up his caffeinated legs, through his torso, and over and around the balls and sockets of the four extra joints he seems to have in each arm. As his left hand descends into his trouser pocket, his legs shuck and jive, and his right hand buzzes from belt buckle, to lapel, to hat brim, to left elbow, and back to lapel before resting on his hip just long enough to counterbalance the weight of the change being extracted from the opposite pocket. The coins hit the counter right as the bartender swoops in to deliver espresso shot number two.

***

"Bite...pain...choke...a lot?"

I reel my stare back to across-the-table distance. Unlike the other women in the café, Kate's not wearing makeup. Her skin is winter break–pale, made even more so by her short black hair. With the sun on her freckles, she looks younger than she did five and a half years ago on the day we were married. "What was that?" I ask.

"I said, 'Do you want a bite of *pain au chocolat*?'" She goes back to her needles and wool.

"You can have it," I say.

"I'm not hungry." *Pull yarn.*

"Look. I can tell you're not fine, so do you want to talk about it or—"

"Not really." *Wrap around.*

"But what—"

"It's nothing, Joe." *Push through.*

"Then why—"

"See, if you don't know, then that's part of the problem." *Yank off.*

"Don't know what? What are you talking about?"

Kate's needles stop cold. "Did you mean what you said last night?"

Last night: French graffiti etched into wooden tables, the words worn smooth by palm sweat and spillover beer. Puke and piss in a urinal stall that wouldn't stop rolling back and forth. Garbage-strewn streets on the long walk back to our 30.00 € hotel.

I take a slurp of coffee and drop the cup down on the saucer, maybe a little too heavily. "What did I say?"

"Never mind," she says.

"How can I know if I meant it, if I don't remember what I said?"

"Now isn't a good time."

"Huh?"

"'Now isn't a good time.' That's what you said."

"A good time for what?"

Kate looks me right in the eyes. "C'mon, Joe," she says.

"What? Do you have something to tell me?"

"Would it matter if I did?"

***

The Bum-Dandy lights a Gitane cigarette and turns away from the bar to face the tables. He's sporting a maroon tie, but it's not around his neck. His conventionally worn tie, his *neck*tie, is blue with gold fleurs-de-lis, but this maroon one is tucked into his breast pocket, doing the jaunty work of a kerchief. He's also wearing two belts.

The first is dressy and black, and it snakes around his waistline. The other is down below his hips. It's brown with a big, country-western buckle, all rhinestones and chrome. Dangling from his right hand is a small, twine-handled shopping bag that in some past life might have carried a jewelry box—a buttery case that promised to snap open to pledges of love and honor and such. Today the crumpled bag is grimy from his cigarette-ashed hands, and it looks like it might contain a scraggily toothbrush or a pair of soiled underpants. But the Bum-Dandy reaches into the bag and takes out a fistful of white tissue paper loosely tied with a red ribbon. He holds the package gently. At the edges. The half-smoked cigarette rests in the corner of his mouth as he pulls the ribbon tight. A wisp of smoke seeps through his lips and is immediately drawn in by his nostrils. Having secured the package to his satisfaction, he looks around the bar, slowly, as if taking an inventory. His eyes meet mine, and he drops the package into the bag. He shoots me an espresso-stained smile. I'm worried that he has caught me sizing him up.

***

"So *are* you, Kate?" I take a bite of the chocolate croissant after all—a calculated attempt to appear nonchalant.

"I'm not." She turns her wedding ring in slow circles around her finger. "But what would you say?"

"If you were?"

"Yeah."

"I'd say, 'Oh my god. Great. Fantastic. Let's celebrate.'"

"Last night you said, 'Now's not a good time.'"

I rub my eyes with the heels of my hands and think about our lives back home in Columbus: the two of us in grad school, both with student loans, living in our cramped apartment. "But you *weren't* last night."

"I'm not now."

"Right. Good." I lick a flake of pastry from the corner of my mouth.

"There's never a good *time*, you know. There's only the time you either decide to or decide not to."

"Then why now?" I say. I'm stirring the dregs of my coffee with the miniature spoon. "Why all these hypothetical—"

"It's not hypothetical."

"But you're *not*."

She jabs her knitting needles into the air for emphasis. "That's not the point."

"What's the point, then?"

"The point is you don't know *what* you want. You think you do, but—"

"What do you mean? I've said all along—"

"Now I don't even know if—" Kate sets the needles down on the table and runs her fingers over her forehead and temples. "I'm just tired, Joe. I'm just really tired."

"You're always tired."

***

The Bum-Dandy drags his Gitane down to the filter, drops the butt into his espresso shot, and gathers himself as if to leave. He pats down his pockets, and nodding *adieu* to nobody in particular, he points himself toward the front door. His legs fold and un-fold. He dances his Bum-Dandy dance. But before he reaches the exit, he shudders to a stop—right beside Kate and me. All his greasy pistons and gears grind down to zero, and he just stands there with his bag in his hand, looking into the space between us.

He clears his throat and gestures through the window. "Regardez là-bas," he says. *Look over there.* His voice is like wet coffee grounds.

We turn and look. Christmastime in the Place des Abbesses. Bells ring in the tower of Saint-Jean l'Evangéliste church. Fur-coated women with big, black sunglasses and architectural heels manipulate the stairs of the Metro stop. A gaggle of tourists marches up the hill toward the Sacré Coeur.

Then I see what he must be pointing toward: a carousel, golden in the sun. Five or six kids with puffy jackets scatter from horse to horse trying to land a prize stallion. The littlest ones are boosted up onto their mounts by parents who give last-minute words of encouragement.

And they're off.

The ride lurches forward. Tiny mittens clutch plastic-molded reins. Scarves become riding crops, lashing at sinew and bone in an effort to eke out just a little more speed as horses and jockeys disappear 'round the backstretch. The parents hover in small groups with their hands in their pockets. They smoke and gossip and plan the business of the day. They shake their heads and mutter at the headlines. They check their watches, worried that they've missed their trains. And the carousel spins and spins. This is a race won by everyone and no one.

The Bum-Dandy lets out a long breath. "C'est magnifique," he says, and he looks down into Kate's lap. "Que faites-vous?" *What are you making?*

Kate wraps the half-scarf around her neck and rubs her arms in a fake shiver.

"Ahhhh…un écharpe," says the Bum-Dandy. *A scarf.* He purses his lips to let Kate know he's impressed. "C'est très bonne." *It's very nice.*

"Un écharpe?" she says, trying the word on for size.

"Oui. Parfait."

Kate raises the needles and the skein of wool. "Knitting," she says, miming a few stitches. "Comment dit-on en Français?" *How do you say this in French?*

"Crochet," he says, bending his index finger into the shape of a crochet hook. Then he shakes his head and frowns. "Non…non." His eyes widen. "Tricoter! Oui, je pense qu'il est le mot. *Tricoter*."

"Tricoter."

"Exactement, madame." He smiles from Kate to me and back again. "Tricoter."

I reach over and rub the back of Kate's hand with my thumb. I turn toward the Bum-Dandy and nod to say, *I understand. Thank you*.

And then he steps away. But he doesn't leave the cafe. He heads back to his spot at the bar, back to his cup and saucer. "Tricoter!" he says, loud enough to be heard over the laughter and the arguments and the clinking of forks and knives and Stella Artois glasses. Looking down into his cup, he snorts at the cigarette filter soaking up the last sip of espresso, and he tucks his shopping bag into his suit pocket.

I hope whatever is in that package is clean and new. A porcelain ballerina. A miniature Formula 1 car. A gift for someone who will come running when this man shows up at the door.

—*2007*

The Get Down

I was the only white kid at the birthday party. The host was one of my first-grade classmates, and we were all sitting at his dining room table, urging him to make quick work of the candles. Because this was 1975, the guys wore hair that was an inch deep, minimum. The girls were braided and beaded, doyennes of the double dutch. With my bowl-cut bangs, I was the odd boy out, which, given that I was the only pale-skinned person in the first grade and one of a handful in the whole elementary, seemed to be the natural order of things.

We scarfed the cake and ice cream, and while the host's mom cleaned up the plates, a teenager—maybe a sister, maybe an aunt—shepherded the ten or so of us kids into the front room, where more members of the family—brothers, cousins, uncles—were drinking beer and smoking cigarettes. The sister/aunt recruited one of the men to help her lift the coffee table out of the way, and then she arranged us in a loose circle in the center of the room. Wearing a jumpsuit and standing on platform heels, she towered toward the ceiling like a disco goddess.

"Now," she said, "guess what time it is." Snapping her fingers, she shook her way over to the record player and then spun back to face us. She was holding the 7-inch single of the Jackson 5's "Dancing Machine."

We cheered. The Jackson 5 was everybody's favorite group. "Dancing Machine" was everybody's favorite song.

"It's time," she said, twisting her polyestered hips lower and lower until she was sitting on the backs of her heels, "to get *down*."

As she slid the disc from the sleeve, I was plugged in and ready, all set to show everybody—my classmates, the sister/aunt, the whole block—that I *was* the dancing machine. Automatic, systematic.

Four years earlier, my peacenik parents had moved us from Texas to here in the Franklin Park section of Columbus, Ohio, an inner-city neighborhood of formerly grand Victorians and Queen Annes, most of which had, by the '70s, fallen into disrepair. Some had been chopped into apartments. Our house wasn't massive, but it was whole, and because of its stone exterior and stained glass windows, it looked to my sister Jill and me like a castle. Across the street was Franklin Park itself, and on summer evenings, Jill and I would sit on our front steps and watch the neighborhood hustlers cruise the park in their Eldorados and Continentals. From the open windows of these big American boats came "Low Rider" and "Keep on Truckin'" and "Living for the City." My parents were partial to Joan Baez and Simon and Garfunkel, so we didn't listen to R&B or funk at home, but still I knew these songs by heart. By osmosis.

The one album Jill and I owned was the Jackson 5's *Greatest Hits*. Jill swore she would one day marry Michael. I wanted to be him, to literally *become* him, grow new skin, sprout new hair. But first I needed to prove I was worthy of Jackson-ness by mastering Michael's dance steps, the ones I'd seen him perform on *Soul Train* and *The Carol Burnett Show*. When nobody was looking, I'd stand in front of my mom's full-length mirror practicing my moves. In my reflection, I could see that I wasn't quite as good as Michael, but I was better than Tito. About on par with Marlon: Rhythmatic, acrobatic.

***

Now at the party, I heard the click-woosh of the record dropping to the turntable. The pops and crackles as the needle struck vinyl. This was my chance to step out of my parents' bedroom and onto the public stage. Right here I would cement my place in the first grade, not as the odd boy out but as the super-bad boy in. Recognizing the significance of the moment, however, caused me to hesitate, and by the time the Jacksons finished singing the opening hook—*Dancing (x3)*—the other kids were already grooving, while I remained stalled in place. Standing there, watching my loose-limbed classmates stick and move, I saw for the first time how plodding even my best steps were. Nothing I had ever performed for the mirror looked half as smooth. These kids weren't just dancing; they were shake-shake-shaking their booties. They were elastic, like the rubbery soul-brothers and -sisters in the image featured in the closing credits of *Good Times*, which I would later learn was an Ernie Barnes painting called "Sugar Shack." They were hip and funky—half-scale versions of the Franklin Park Cadillac cruisers. When practicing at the mirror, how had I not seen that whatever I was, I certainly wasn't, well, *this*? How had I not noticed my oppositeness?

That's when I understood that I had mistaken desire for skill.

I stood frozen for at least a minute before the sister/aunt smiled and said, "Aww, that's cute. He shy," which drew a few laughs from the beer drinkers on the periphery. She placed her palm against the small of my back as if trying to coax rhythm into me. "It's okay, baby. Just do what you feel."

I felt like going home, but I knew it wasn't time for my mom to pick me up. I could sense that people were staring at me—not the kids, who were too busy trying to impress each other to be concerned with whatever I was doing or not doing, but the older folks. And I realized that the longer I just stood there, the longer I'd be the center of attention. So I started moving—dancing, sort of. I planted my right foot and stepped with my left. Then I planted my left foot and stepped with my right. Plant, step. Plant, step. Jacksonesque it wasn't, but at least I was keeping the beat.

"That's it, baby," the sister/aunt said. "You got it." Then she started moving back and forth with me. Plant, step. "Come on, y'all," she said, and she pulled two of the beer drinkers off the couch and onto the floor. Next she waded into the pool of elbows and knees that was my fellow first graders, and soon she had all of them imitating me. The whole room. Adults and kids. We were moving as one.

I know the sister/aunt meant well, but there's no harsher critique than to witness a grand production of your own incompetence. Watching those unencumbered bodies get handcuffed to me and my rigidity seemed almost an act of cruelty, like hobbling Dr. J or muzzling Muhammad Ali.

The honky-tonk line dance lasted only a few seconds before one boy broke free and transitioned to a near-perfect imitation of Michael Jackson's signature robot routine. This kid truly was a dancing machine, and he made my unintentionally robotic steps look even more pedestrian. But thankfully he'd steered the room's attention away from me. I'd never been so happy to be forgotten.

***

That birthday party turned out to be to the first of many steps that would distance me from those kids and from that neighborhood. The next year, in second grade, I attended a private Montessori school that was almost entirely white. The year after that, my dad, who had been directing the state agency that advocated for people with disabilities, took a similar job at the national level, and my family moved to Montgomery County, Maryland, one of the wealthiest counties in the United States. As we drove away from Franklin Park, I wasn't sad to leave. Our house had been broken into several times; an arsenal of rocks had been chucked through our stained glass; one day while I was waiting for the bus that would take me to my new private school, a group of older boys shook me down for my lunch money. Beyond all that, I was sick of being called *honky*.

After a year in Maryland, we moved back to Columbus, where my dad was now directing a vocational rehabilitation facility. This time my parents bought a cookie-cutter house in a suburb called Worthington, which was as lily-white as the name sounds. We lived there all through the Reagan '80s, and in middle and high school, every time I heard an upper-class white kid use the n-word or tell a black joke, I'd shake my head at his ignorance, and I'd silently thank my parents for having given me the gift of living in Franklin Park.

But I wasn't thankful solely for the cultural awareness I'd gleaned—no, I wasn't that goodhearted. I was also betting that the years I'd spent in a black neighborhood, or "the ghetto," as I'd taken to calling it by then, would make me seem more hard-edged and complex than I would have been otherwise. None of my Worthington friends had ever run their fingertips around the milky circumference of a whitewall tire, as I had on a few of those Franklin Park Caddies and Lincolns. None of them had ever been humbled at a black kid's birthday party.

After I got my license, I'd sometimes drive my buddies across town to Franklin Park, ostensibly under the guise of showing them my family's old stone house, so different from the aluminum siding that encased much of Worthington. Really, though, I wanted them to notice all the *other* houses in the neighborhood. The boarded-up windows. The security bars. I wanted them to appreciate the Schlitz Malt Liquor billboards and the shady-looking taverns. I knew how these urban details would play to a suburban audience, and I was more than happy to accept any residual badassness my once having lived in the inner city would bring.

In the '90s, Franklin Park and the adjacent community, Olde Towne East, underwent the now-familiar pattern of gentrification. Gays and urban professionals, black and white, renovated the Victorians and Queen Annes, and many of the mansions that had been carved into apartments were rehabbed back to stateliness. Tension arose between the newcomers and the longstanding homeowners. (The complicated interactions and competing agendas among Olde Towne East residents were documented in the 2003 film *Flag Wars*.) I didn't—and still don't—know exactly how I feel about gentrification, but I knew one thing for sure: As soon as Franklin Park turned "nice," there was no longer any reason for me to drag my friends there.

***

Kate and I are now raising our young son and daughter in a small town in South Carolina, where we both teach college. When we shop at the Food Lion or visit the public library, I see a higher density of dark-skinned faces than at any time since those seven years I lived in Franklin Park. I'm proud to reside amid such diversity, but I sometimes worry that I value living in a racially mixed community primarily so that I can applaud myself *for* valuing it. The worst kind of liberal self-congratulations: *Look at me! I live among actual black people!* And then there's this: I don't really live among black people. The town may be nearly 40% black, but our neighborhood is nearly 100% white.

On those rare occasions when I find myself on the black side of town, I think about my parents and their decision to buy a house in a neighborhood where they knew they'd be in the minority. My mom and dad have always preached equality and acceptance, but lots of well-meaning people—liberal or otherwise—can talk up the importance of these lofty ideals. My parents didn't just talk; they put their mortgage where their mouths were. They put their *kids* where their mouths were. For seven years, they enlisted Jill and me in the fight to erode the racial divide. I feel like a hypocritical coward by comparison. For all my progressive politics, I know I'm not going to move my kids into a house across town. I know I'm not going to send them to a school across town. We drive through the black neighborhood, but we don't stop.

My son will be starting kindergarten in the fall, so I've been thinking a lot about neighborhoods and schools, and what makes the so-called good ones "good" and the so-called bad ones "bad." I recently downloaded the Zillow app so I can research properties in a subdivision (*plantation* is often the appellation of choice for developers here in South Carolina) that would put our kids in an elementary with higher test scores than the school they are currently zoned to attend. As you can probably guess, this subdivision is even whiter and richer than the neighborhood we live in now. When I'm snooping on Zillow, I feel ashamed—almost dirty, like I've been looking at Internet porn. But why should I feel anything but conscientious? Isn't the move to "good" schools the kind of decision "good" parents make? Then again, maybe "doing it for the kids" is a cop-out. Maybe I'm using my kids to justify my own desires, prejudices, and cultural assumptions. Maybe *I* want the big house in the ritzy neighborhood; the kids are just the excuse.

***

A few months ago, my dad visited from Ohio to attend my son's fifth birthday party. All the guests were white. There was no dancing. After the cake and ice cream, while the kids were tearing through the yard on a dinosaur egg hunt and my dad and I were garbage-bagging the paper plates, I thought back to the '70s, to that first-grade party, and I wondered what had driven my parents to make the "bad" decision of moving us to the "bad" neighborhood with the "bad" schools. Could they possibly have anticipated that I'd later see my years in Franklin Park as a gift? If so, then how the heck did my mom and dad get so wise and righteous—and why hadn't those genes been handed down to me?

As we cleaned up the kitchen, I told my dad about the research I'd been doing into neighborhoods and schools, and I shared a little of my ambivalence about the prospect of moving to the well-groomed subdivision with the award-winning elementary. "I'm conflicted," I told him. "This is complicated."

"No it isn't," he said.

I felt better already. My dad would apply clarity to my confusion.

"You send your kids to the better school," he said. "That's the answer."

"Really?" I wanted clarity, sure, but I was anticipating a little more nuance with my clarity. Or maybe I was expecting my dad to be clear in the opposite direction: Don't sell out to the white-centric notion of what's better.

He nodded. And in that nod I could see that this was a calculation he'd been working on for a long time, maybe since I was the age my son is now. He'd already factored in the value of integration and diversity. He'd already accepted as a given the fact that social class is more salient than skin color and that there are many different kinds of "good education." He'd already tallied his accounting of the plusses and minuses of our family's years in Franklin Park. And after considering all of these variables, his solution was *send your kids to the better school*. Period.

This may not have been what I expected my dad to say, but as soon as he said it, I realized it was what I *wanted* him to say. I wanted reassurance from the wise and righteous that it was okay for me to be stalking the subdivision.

The cleanup complete, we cracked open afternoon beers. "The only good investment I ever made," my dad said, "was in you kids."

I understood that in one respect he meant *investment* literally—racking up credit card debt to pay my college tuition, for example. But I also knew that he didn't mean it only literally. I knew that what he was really saying was, "I love you. I'm proud of you. You're a good dad." And yet, those words, "good investment," got me wondering about the opposite, my dad's *bad* investments. And that got me thinking again about the inner city.

"Hey, Dad," I said, "Let me ask you something. Did you and mom buy that Franklin Park house because you thought it was important for Jill and me to grow up in a diverse environment?" I took a long sip from my beer. "Or was it because you thought the house was a potential investment, that you'd be able to buy low while the neighborhood was down and then sell high when it turned around?"

"Mostly the second one," he said. "The investment."

I'm not sure if I was surprised or relieved to learn that my dad was just as imperfect as I am. The belief that our parents' motivations and decisions are purer than ours—that they are wiser and more righteous than us—is a myth. But it's the myth upon which the institution of parenthood is built.

"Did you actually make money?" I asked him.

"Not much," he said. "A few thousand dollars. Just enough for the down payment on the house in Maryland."

My peacenik parents, it turns out, were OGs. Original Gentrifiers. And like me on that birthday party dance floor, they were out of synch with the rhythm of the neighborhood. They got to Franklin Park twenty years early for the big payoff—if profit was their primary objective, and I don't believe it was, regardless of what my dad says about seeing the house as an investment. Still, whatever induced my parents to move to Franklin Park, my childhood was richer for the time I spent there.

I looked through the window to the yard, where a gaggle of kids in cone-shaped party hats was hunting for dino eggs. I saw my son and two-year-old daughter moving with shameless spasms of joy each time somebody unearthed another treasure. Wherever Kate and I eventually decide to live, whatever school we send our kids to, I hope they'll continue to move through life as they move now: unbidden and unconstrained. I hope they won't worry too much when they find themselves the odd kids out. I hope they won't feel entitled when they find themselves the cool kids in. I hope they'll, what? *Dance like nobody's watching?* Nah. That's the trite chorus to a country song. Sounds like a lyric cross-stitched to a throw pillow. Though I fully endorse the sentiment, I don't want to saddle my kids with that specific diction and syntax any more than I wanted to bind my first-grade classmates to my timid two-step. Instead, what I wish for my son and daughter is this: When it comes time to get down, I hope they'll shake their asses right on down.

—2016

Simpatico

I've been driving a cargo van down a Mexican two-lane for eleven teeth-clenching hours. Kate is trying to keep me alert by playing Berlitz Basic Spanish cassettes on a boom box, but it's past midnight and I'm losing concentration, hypnotized by the rhythm of the windshield wipers. I've squinted through the Econoline's dull headlights for so long my face hurts. We're on the coastal highway, somewhere between Mazatlán and Tepic, and the night is a few clicks darker than those back home in Columbus. I steer into s-curves and around potholes—*baches* in Spanish, Kate tells me—with just enough high beam to see that thick jungle brush flanks the road. By day this place would be beautiful. Pulsing and green. But I'm too tired to appreciate the scenery. And I long ago stopped repeating the nouns prompted by the Berlitz tape: *coche* and *reloj* and *playa*. Kate pronounces them alone. For several miles, hers is the only live voice in the van. Eventually I ask her how to say *I need a bathroom and a big coffee.*

The Lonely Planet has us believing that by night Mexican roads are patrolled by crooked cops and car-jacking banditos. And in my semi-lucid daze, I hear the voice of a friend from work: *You know, my cousin's buddy drove through Mexico. He was just sitting at a stoplight, when somebody slid up beside him and hacked off his left hand. Just to get his freaking watch. And it was a Timex!* My work friend is an alarmist, with one eye ever tuned to cable news. But I don't want to tempt potential watch thieves by stopping to pee at a seedy cantina. So while Kate takes a flashlight to the Rand McNally, I hunt for a stop that meets our American expectations for highway safety. On my Citizen wristwatch, I clock fifteen minutes with no evidence of commercial life. Then I finally spot the green, red, and white sign beaming above the palm trees: PEMEX. Mexico's national gas monopoly.

We pull onto a gravel drive that opens to gas pumps and a 7-Eleven-style quick mart. The store's cheerfully franchised exterior clashes with the tropical surroundings, and it seems to be sweating—as if someone shipped the whole place down from a Minneapolis suburb and uncrated it here in the jungle heat. The windows are so fogged with condensation, we can't see inside.

I aim for a spot near the entrance, and I throw the van into park. Through the cracked windshield, I see five dark-skinned men leaning against the front doors, under a lip of roof and out of the rain. I can't tell if they're in their thirties or forties, but with their muddy jeans and work shirts, it's clear they've spent their lives doing jobs that leave calluses. They're all lean as Bantamweights. Even from ten yards away, I can see the veins in their forearms. Crushed Tecate cans litter the ground.

"Let's keep going," I say, shifting into reverse.

Kate hits stop on the boom box. "You wanted coffee."

"I can wait." As I curl the van backward, our headlights shine directly on the men. They all look our way. One of them lowers the bill of his ball cap. Another shields his eyes with his hand, then goes back to cleaning his fingernails with what looks like a pocketknife. I'm wondering if they can see us inside the van. I'm about to drive off when I notice the blankets and bedrolls at their feet. "Jesus, Kate. Those guys are sleeping here."

She nods. "Maybe they're migrants. On their way north."

"They're a long way from north."

I check the odometer and know exactly how far they have to go.

Kate and I left Columbus a month ago. We moved out of our apartment, put our furniture in storage, and loaded Watershed's Econoline with camping gear and canned food. Our plan is to spend three or four months on the road, going as deep into Mexico as we can before the money runs out. We've done some traveling in the three years we've been married but never for this long. This time our mailing address is a PO Box. We're like a shadowy offshore corporation.

When we get home, Kate'll be starting her PhD in British Literature. I quit my miserable office job the week we left, so other than the band, I don't know what I'll be driving back to. The odometer tells me I'm three-thousand miles from Columbus. Three-thousand miles from having to interview for another soul-sucking job. The five Mexicans are nine-hundred miles from the border. They're going north looking for work. I'm headed south, avoiding it.

***

His nails sufficiently manicured, Pocketknife folds the blade into his jeans. Then he bends over and scrapes up a handful of gravel. He showers the other men with tiny rocks. Everybody ducks, elbows to ears. They laugh as they straighten, and they pass around more beer.

"How far to Tepic?" I say. I'm thinking ahead to a soft bed and morning coffee.

Kate scans the map. I try to shift gears, but the stick won't go into drive.

"What's wrong?" she says.

I shift back to park and start over: reverse—neutral—nothing.

"Transmission's locked," I say. I try coaxing the shifter into drive. Try applying steady pressure. Try jerking it. Nothing works. I try again and again, but the transmission won't budge.

Not knowing what else to do, I pedal the gas, and we circle around the lot. Backwards. I take us through a 360-degree O-turn, and the headlights again flood the Mexicans. They give us a second look, and I notice that Pocketknife is wearing sandals made from tire treads.

"All we've got is reverse?" Kate says, wrinkling her brow.

I stab the shifter to the left. "And park."

We idle there, the rain smacking the van like the sky had let loose with a bag of marbles. It's loud, it's hot, and we don't have air-conditioning. Roll the windows down, and we get wet. Leave them up, and we steam. We roll the windows halfway down.

Though my side window, I see two PEMEX attendants squatting on the oily concrete. One rests an elbow on a gas pump; the other, wearing a New York Yankees cap, gestures toward us. I wonder what we look like to him: two gringos rolling their elephantine van in backward circles. Yankee Cap hops on a BMX bike and rides our way.

I turn to Kate. "How do you say mechanic?"

She holds up the boom box. "It's on tape three," she says. Then she opens the door and climbs down to meet the guy.

We dated for ten years before we married, so I've been with Kate long enough to know that she deals with strangers better than I do. For me social situations are like business transactions—polite but curt. Everybody likes Kate. She's funny, smart, and pretty. My shaved head and Eastern-bloc cheekbones make me look like I'm plotting a hate crime.

Yankee Cap's uniform stretches from neck to ankles, and as he smiles, I can see the silver caps on his teeth. "You need a mechanic?" he asks Kate in mildly accented English.

I step down from the van to join them. Yankee Cap says his name is Chiclet, like the gum. He's about thirty and way too stocky for such a tiny bike. His knees almost hit the handlebars. He tells us there's a garage a kilometer or so up the road, and he volunteers to call the local mechanic to see if he can make it out.

"Tonight?" I say. "In the rain?"

Chiclet takes off his cap and pushes a few fingers through his slick hair. "I don't know, amigo. Let me call and see." He pedals toward the phone.

I'm conflicted. Like Blanche DuBois, we're depending on the kindness of strangers. And yet an American-bred suspicion has kicked in. A miniature Uncle Sam has appeared on my shoulder, whispering that *they* want what's ours and they'll steal it if they have to. I look over to the c-store at the five migrants who surely think Kate and I are wealthy because we can afford to be here. I'm worried that they see us as materialistic, self-important Americans even as I'm typecasting them as shifty, conniving Mexicans. But I'm not like that, am I? A xenophobe? I'm pretty sure I'm just suspicious of do-gooders. Even home in Ohio I wonder, *what's this guy's angle?* when faced with Good Samaritanism. I have a hard time believing anyone would help us simply because we need help. Maybe paranoia is a by-product of privilege. But I can't afford that brand of fear tonight. It's trust Chiclet or nothing. Still, I'll keep an eye on him. He's a Yankee fan. You can't trust them.

Chiclet rides back smiling, saying the mechanic is on the way. And sure enough, twenty minutes later a pick-up truck pulls into the lot. With Chiclet acting as translator, the mechanic climbs into the van to try the gear shifter. Now I feel awful about leaving the windows half-open. The driver's seat is torn, and the exposed cushioning has soaked up the rain like a Nerf football, but the mechanic doesn't seem to notice. I'm still convinced that with just the right touch, drive might be had. He starts the engine, palms the shifter, and pulls forward and down. Reverse—neutral—no such luck.

To Plan B: The mechanic opens the hood and holds the end of a dipstick to his nose.

"Transmission fluid," Chiclet says.

As the mechanic wipes the stick and slides it back into the pan, Kate and I turn to each other, crossing our fingers. Even I know a pint of fluid is cheaper than a whole new transmission. He pauses for dramatic effect and then pulls out the dipstick. It reads right in the crosshatch, midway between min and max.

The mechanic says something to Chiclet and points under the van, and I reach into the cargo space for my beach towel. It's clear that the terry cloth won't be much insulation from the muddy gravel, but to be polite the mechanic unfolds the towel and drapes it over the puddles anyway. After poking and prodding under the chassis, he crawls out with the prognosis.

"He'll come back tomorrow and tow you to his garage," says Chiclet.

"Does he know what the problem is?" I say.

Chiclet pulls a bandanna from his back pocket and tosses it to the mechanic.

"The problem, amigo," he says, "is that your transmission is fucked."

In the morning, the mechanic will rebuild the tranny and get us back on the road. How much will he charge us? That's tomorrow's problem. Tonight's problem is that we're sleeping in the van, in a gas station, in the jungle.

"Could be worse," Kate says. "We could be stuck out on the road."

She's right, of course. I imagine the two of us pushing the van into the brush, hoping the *Federales* will find us before the banditos do.

"We need to celebrate," she says. "Let's get some beer." Kate's always up for a party, sometimes to the point of annoyance. Right now I'd rather crawl into the van and go to sleep, making the morning come faster.

I look back to the store, where the five Mexicans are illuminated in the fluorescence. "Celebrate what?"

Kate shakes her head, turns, and walks away.

We've been fighting since Flagstaff. Two weeks ago, at the Route 66 International Hostel, we walked into the lounge, where four backpackers were practicing trick shots on the pool table. One of them was using *Let's Go—USA* as a coaster for his beer. He wasn't American: He wore his jeans too high on the hips. But he was blessed with the veteran traveler's ability to look not of a place and yet completely at home there.

Kate asked him if she could borrow the book. "I want to see what they wrote about my hometown."

"You are from here," he said. I couldn't tell if it was a statement or a question. He swigged his beer and handed the *Let's Go* to her. "From what city?"

She flipped through the pages. "Columbus, Ohio."

"Like Christopher Columbus?"

"Exactly."

He said he was from Paris. While Kate explained how much we loved France, I went to buy beer, leaving her with Paris and his hostel buddies. When I came back they were standing around the pool table, watching as Kate tried to jump the cue ball over the eight. Soon everyone was drunk. I played DJ on the jukebox. Kate danced with Paris. The guy was a shitty dancer, but she was having fun.

A few songs later, we all staggered to a dance club, where Paris disappeared into a swarm of sorority girls. I took Kate by the hand, and we conga'd out to the floor. And I was feeling it. I was the white James Brown. One-hundred-fifty pounds of pink-skinned soul. Kate put her hands on my hips. But she wasn't dancing with me so much as pointing me in the right direction.

"What's wrong?" I said over the *Bumpf-Bumpf-Bumpf* of the music.

"You're not with the beat." She took my waist and tried to show me.

I pulled away. "What do you mean?" How could I not be with the beat? I'm a bass player. Rhythm is my job.

"You're just swaying back and forth."

"But it's 4/4 time. Left-right-left-right."

"You're not moving *with* me. You're not dancing *with* me."

"Then count it out for me."

Her voice broke as she strained over the volume. "I don't know how to count it. You've got to *feel* it."

"Can't we just dance?" I yelled. "Without a goddamn rhythm lesson?"

"Try to move your hips like this—"

I pushed her away. "You didn't show Paris how to dance."

"But he's a good dancer."

"How!" I was screaming.

"Some people just have it," she said, and she turned away.

I grabbed her. "I have rhythm. I'm in a band."

"Maybe that's why you guys never made it!" she yelled. "Maybe you're not that good." She slowed down to emphasize not...that...good.

I came up short of breath and turned toward the dance floor. Paris was deep in the throng. "He's better than me? How?" I reached for Kate's shoulder. "How!"

But Kate was all icy detachment. "Don't touch me," she said. And she walked away.

I followed her out of the bar and right into a group of police officers. They'd been slumping casually against their mountain bikes, but as soon as they saw Kate and the tears that were now sliding down her face, they went to work.

First job, separate me from Kate. One cop took me by the elbow and led me ten yards down the street. "You want to tell me what happened?" he said. He was fit, with calves like canned hams. The product of a thousand uphill miles on the Flagstaff bicycle beat. Where donut jokes go to die.

In his eyes, I was the asshole who abuses his girlfriend, and anything I said would only reinforce my assholeness. "Nothing," I said. "Seriously."

"Then why is your girlfriend crying?"

"She's not my girlfriend." I looked back to where two cops were consoling Kate. One of them was asking her, "Was he dancing with another girl?"

"No," Kate said, sobbing. "He was trying to dance with *me*."

"She's my wife," I said, turning back to my cop. "And she's crying because she thinks I can't dance."

"You can't dance?" he said.

"She *thinks* I can't dance."

He took a ballpoint from his pocket and clicked it a few times. "Hmmm…" Then he tapped the pen on the handlebars. "Have you ever thought about lessons?"

Walking back to the hostel, I tried making up, but Kate was still mad and hurt. She said she was scared of me. She'd never seen me so angry. She said she just wanted to go home. And she didn't mean back to the hostel.

***

Now, approaching the store entrance, I catch up to Kate. We excuse ourselves past the Mexicans, and I'm feeling especially conscious of my whiteness and my baldness. These guys are much younger than they looked earlier. Twenties, tops. They seem curious, possibly ready to fight. Pocketknife smiles as he holds the door open for us.

The store is blindingly well lit. I can see everything and nothing, like leaving a matinee movie by the doors that lead straight into the sunny parking lot. And this is the first significant air conditioning we've felt since we crossed the border. My rain-wet t-shirt feels like it might freeze.

Kate grabs a bag of chips and heads for the beer cooler while I beeline for the door marked *Caballeros*. The bathroom is spotless, and it smells good, like it's been splashed with disinfectant and rosewater. Everything is white on white, fluorescence on porcelain, safe institutional sterility. It smells like home.

I return from the bathroom thinking, Kate's right. This isn't so bad. We've got snacks. Beer. Bathrooms. This is practically my living room on football Saturday.

But I can't find Kate. She's not by the beer coolers. She's not in the snack aisle. She's not at the register. I figure she must be in the *Senoritas'* room, so I wait there a few minutes. But we're three-thousand miles from home. With no cell phones and no GPS. All we've got is a van that runs backward. So I can't wait. I knock on the door of the bathroom. No answer. I try the knob. It's unlocked, so I nudge it open. There's nobody inside.

I go to the windows, trying to see if she walked back to the van. But they're too fogged-over. I wipe half circles with my palm and press my face up to the glass, cupping my hands to my forehead to shield out the light. But I still can't see. The condensation is on the outside.

Then I remember the Mexicans. Mean-eyed drifters that want what's mine. They'll steal it if they have to. I hustle toward the front door, and push it open with both hands.

No Kate. No Mexicans. No bedrolls.

Nothing but the night.

Then I hear her voice. She's working through the Spanish words, practicing them out loud, just as she's been doing for nine-hundred miles. "Buenas noches, Señors."

I turn and see Kate. Standing with the Mexicans, who've moved twenty feet down the side of the building. They're laughing, Kate and these men. She holds a six-pack in one hand. The other hand is extended toward Pocketknife, who gingerly shakes it. His forearm is marked with scars and home-inked tattoos.

I've known Kate for thirteen years, and I don't know her at all. If I can't grasp the complexities of one person, how can I ever measure the subtleties and variances of an entire country? I'll never know them and what they want.

Kate looks over to me, smiles, and says, "Want a beer?"

Pocketknife smiles too. "Bienvenido, amigo," he says. And it hits me that when Kate and I entered the store, the Mexicans must have broken camp so as not to block the doors. But in doing so, they moved farther from the air-conditioning spilling from them.

I motion for Pocketknife to come back to the entrance, back to where it's cool. But he shrugs as if to say one place is as good as any other.

So I walk toward him. And toward Kate. Closing the space between them and us.

She hands me a beer, and as promised, we celebrate. Beneath the convenience store overhang, sheltered from the rain, we drink the sweating jungle and dance the lonely highway rhythms. Kate, five Mexican guys, and me. All of us on the way to someplace else.

—2008

In Any August

August 9, 2005. US Route 64. East of Tarboro, NC.

The pre-dawn highway is an artery swimming with pock-marked amphetamine addicts, puttin'-the-hammer-down truckers, dirty-nailed lovers, and me.

I'm driving a van of sleeping musicians to a gig in a resort town. In three long hours, the rising sun will appear in my windshield, but right now two fast-approaching high beams from the west-bound lanes have me squinting. We're speeding toward each other at a combined 140 miles per hour, offset only by the faith we put in those two yellow lines. He barrels past with a Doppler whine and then disappears from the side-view mirror. I wonder where he's headed at 3:17 on a Tuesday morning.

Six hundred miles northwest of here, my sister and her husband are trying to sleep on hospital recliners in the NICU. I grip the steering wheel with both hands, hoping my two-pound nephews are stronger than the virus that has infiltrated their blood streams.

August 9, 2005. Kingston, TN.

Tennessee Department of Corrections Officers Wayne "Cotton" Morgan and Larry Harris escort George Hyatte across the parking lot of the Roane County Courthouse. Hyatte is two years into a thirty-five-year stretch for assault and armed robbery. He appeared in court this morning to enter a guilty plea on an unrelated robbery charge. As Officers Morgan and Harris lead the cuffed and shackled Hyatte into the van that will take him back to the Brushy Mountain Correction Complex, Hyatte jerks free from their grasp and yells, "Shoot him!"

Morgan and Harris turn to see Hyatte's wife, Jennifer, steadying a 9mm pistol from thirteen feet away. *Crack.* Officer Morgan thuds to the pavement, a bullet wound in his stomach. Officer Harris exchanges shots with Jennifer Hyatte as she backs toward her Ford Explorer. Meanwhile, George Hyatte crawls to the Explorer's open passenger door. Harris empties his weapon into the SUV, his sixth shot shattering the driver's side window. He starts to reload, but then reaches down and unholsters Morgan's pistol. Harris gets off five shots from his wounded partner's gun as George and Jennifer Hyatte speed toward Interstate 40. They disappear into the Tennessee morning.

An hour later, Cotton Morgan dies at the University of Tennessee Medical Center. A nationwide manhunt begins.

August 9, 2005. Kill Devil Hills, NC.

A hard-bitten wind whips across the Outer Banks, making this midsummer evening feel like early May. Somewhere behind the homes-on-stilts that line the Intracoastal Waterway, the sun is cut in half by the horizon.

My bandmates and I are all denim and leather, black boots and dark jeans. Surely we stand out amid the nylon and Gore-Tex everyone else in this beachfront bar is wearing. The band is called Watershed, and the program director from the local radio station and his girlfriend have brought us here to drink Budweisers from buckets. Cold beer on the beach. These are the moments that tell us we are not fools to leave our wives and kids home in Columbus as we log hundreds of thousands of miles in the van. Still, every fifteen minutes or so I check my cell phone for news from the hospital. A week ago, my sister Jill gave birth to fraternal twins, ten weeks prematurely. She and her husband are now living at Riverside Methodist, breathing hard against the incubator glass, willing their sons into the world.

I flag the waitress for more beer, and as she walks past the stage to the kitchen, I see Tommy, our barely adequate guitar player, asking the kid who has been singing beach bar standards like "Brown Eyed Girl" and "Cheeseburger in Paradise" if he can borrow the guitar to play a tune. Tommy shoulders the kid's acoustic, picks up the microphone stand, and walks it over to the four women sitting at the picnic table next to me. They are long-legged and lean, with sun-streaked hair and floral sarongs. They smell like Coppertone. They've been ordering margaritas in breezy Virginia drawls.

"I'd like to dedicate this song to these lovely ladies right here," Tommy says, smiling his twenty-four-year-old grin. He's close enough to freshen their drinks.

Tommy's not his real name, but that's what we call him. We borrowed the nickname from Tommy Thayer, the guitarist who has taken over for Ace Frehley in KISS. Our Tommy is a last-minute substitute for our regular guitar player, a guy we call Pooch, who is currently home in Ohio with his very pregnant wife. They are expecting their first child any day. I've never heard Tommy sing, but I suspect his voice is no better than his pedestrian guitar playing.

Tommy strums a few shaky G-chords and then, to my horror, starts to serenade the women from Virginia with Roy Orbison's "Crying," a notoriously difficult song to sing. Bracing for the train wreck, I lean toward the radio guy to explain that Tommy isn't really in the band, but before I can get the words out, radio guy's girlfriend says, "Isn't he adorable?" She's damn near swooning.

I turn around to see Tommy running his index finger down his cheek, pretending to be *cry-eye-eye-eye-ing* over the four Virginians who are now cocking their heads and twirling their hair between their fingers. I look under the table at their pedicured feet and painted nails. Tommy has made their toes curl.

Thirty minutes later, he's shaking tequila-soaked cubes around in a plastic cup; dipping his pale, Midwestern toes in the Atlantic; skimming through low tide with a tanned and toned marketing coordinator from Richmond. The two of them stand with their backs to the ocean, shoes in their hands. Their hair lashes in the wind as they wave up to us on the patio.

They're looking westward, where every day ends, like it or not.

August 9, 1969. 10050 Cielo Drive. Beverly Hills, CA.

"Look, bitch. I have no mercy for you," says twenty-one-year-old Susan Atkins as Sharon Tate begs for her life and the life of her unborn baby. "You're going to die, and you'd better get used to it."

Tate is twenty-six, and she's two weeks from her due date. She is stabbed sixteen times. Voytek Frykowski, Abigail Folger, Jay Sebring, and Steven Parent are also slain by Atkins, Tex Watson, and Patricia Krenwinkel. Before fleeing into the night, Atkins mops Tate's blood with a towel and uses it to smear *PIG* on the front door. Murder is on the tip of the national tongue.

August 10, 2005. Tennessee Highway Patrol, District One Headquarters. Knoxville, TN.

Hundreds of calls come in, but law enforcement officials have no confirmed sightings of George and Jennifer Hyatte. Jennifer has family in Utah, so photos of the two fugitives are faxed and e-mailed to authorities in the North and West. The last time George escaped from prison, he—like so many others who can't seem to fit-in—fled to Florida. South and East.

August 10, 2005. Durham, NC.

The Red Roof Inn at exit 270 sits on the wrong side of Interstate 40, the border between collegiate Chapel Hill and hardscrabble

Durham. Tucked in a grove of slash pines, the hotel is surrounded by so much vegetation that we drive past it twice before we finally notice the dim lobby lights. A few bobtail trucks are parked along the service road. A police cruiser idles at the road's dead end. The mostly dark parking lot is scattered with dinged-up cars. This is where a man goes when he doesn't want to be found.

While the band checks-in, I call Kate. She tells me nothing has changed with the twins. Still in the NICU. Still in the incubator. Wired and IV'd and monitored around the clock. My cell bleeps with another call: Pooch, our guitarist. His wife's water has broken, and they're running out the door.

"Smoke a cigar for us," I say. And I click back to Kate, wondering if *nothing has changed* is good news or bad.

I walk the perimeter of the lot as Kate and I talk. It smells of pine needles and highway exhaust. Behind these hotel room doors are desperate salesmen and battered women and families on their way to Disney World. People are fucking and fighting. They're doing drugs and contemplating suicide. Masturbating to something they'll feel ashamed of later. Worrying over their next move.

Just before she hangs up, Kate says, "Happy birthday, boo."

I turn thirty-six today.

August 10, 1969. Stoughton, WI.

Number one with a bullet: "This is the Dawning of the Age of Aquarius." Joining the Fifth Dimension at the top of the charts are sex and love, murder and war, riots and rockets, peace signs and smiley faces and hippies and Yippies and "Dizzy" by Tommy Roe. This summer the American flag goes up on the moon. This summer Ted Kennedy drives his Delmont 88 and Mary Jo Kopechne off a bridge on Chappaquiddick Island.

On a Sunday morning, I breathe for the first time. The son of an ex-priest and an ex-nun. Five days from Woodstock and less than a month from the My Lai Massacre. Hot Fun in the Summertime.

August 10, 1969. 3301 Waverly Drive. Los Angeles, CA.

Fourteen-year-old Frank Struthers knocks on the door of his mother and stepfather's place. No answer. Strange. His mom and Leno should have gotten back from Lake Isabella last night. The boat is parked out front. The lights are on inside. They must be home. Frank knocks again. Nothing. So he walks to a neighbor's house and calls Suzan, his big sister. She arrives a few minutes later with her boyfriend, Joseph. Suzan watches from the car as Frank and Joseph crawl through a window. They find *DEATH* written in blood across the refrigerator. On a living room wall, red letters read, *DEATH TO PIGS*.

Detectives initially call the murders of Rosemary and Leno LaBianca the work of a copycat killer.

August 10, 2005. Parts Unknown.

George and Jennifer Hyatte met when she was working as a prison nurse. She was fired for sneaking food to him. A few months later, she asked and received permission from the warden to marry George. Friends say they are very much in love.

August 10, 2005. Kingston, TN.

Cotton Morgan is survived by his wife Viann; son Dennis; daughter Carla Sue; and her children, Cole and Hallie. Morgan liked to hunt deer up in the hills near Frozen Head State Park. He also enjoyed helping relatives cut hay and keep bees.

August 10, 2005. Chapel Hill, NC.

"Hey, jackasses. Be cool back there," Biggie says from behind the wheel. "We got a cop behind us."

I take a sip of my Pabst and stick it between my legs. Next to me on the bench seat, Tommy does the same. Six of us—band and road crew—sit straight and tall like kids who've been scolded by their teacher. Biggie's the tour manager, and he hasn't had a drop to drink, but still he keeps his hands at 10:00 and 2:00. Then from behind us: the party lights. Kaleidoscopic flashes of red, white, and blue. A few yelps from the siren.

Biggie eases the van to the curb and digs into his pocket for his wallet. "Guess I missed a turn signal back there."

My stomach sinks. In addition to the beers we're drinking, there's a whole case on ice in the Igloo cooler that's currently lodged between my right leg and the van's side door. Watershed hasn't made any money this tour. A vanload of open-container citations would force us to limp back to Columbus dead broke.

"Gimme your cell numbers," Tommy says, laying a pillow across his lap to hide his PBR, "in case you have to bail me out." He tells us he's currently serving a thirty-day suspended sentence for a DUI. Leaving Ohio is already a violation of his probation, but leaving Ohio and getting busted on an alcohol charge would automatically activate the jail time. "Goddamn," he says, stiff as stone. "I can't spend thirty days in the can."

For a few seconds, we just sit there, silhouetted by the high-watt spotlight firing from behind. Then a gruff voice comes over the loud speaker, "Driver, please exit the vehicle. Slowly. With your hands right where we can see 'em."

Biggie climbs out with his palms forward, squinting into the light, summertime bugs buzzing around his head.

"Quick. Gimme the empties," I say, dropping three cans into the cooler. "I'll stash—"

"Don't fucking move," Tommy grits through his teeth. "They got flashlights all over us."

Through the tinted windows, I see crawling light beams. The van is surrounded by cops, all hitting the van with Maglites from ten or fifteen feet. One of them shouts, "Listen up in there! We need you to open the side door *very* slowly."

The side door is really two doors: the front half swings open to the right, the back half opens to the left. With my right foot, I pin the beer cooler between the seat bench and the back half of the door. Now, when I pop open the front half, the cooler will remain hidden, but if the cops ask us to open up the back, a case of Pabst and seven pounds of ice will surely spill to their feet.

Tommy sucks a breath as I push the door open.

These aren't cops; they're commandos. Decked out in tactical uniforms and duty boots. With coal-black pistols and bulletproof vests. They look like soldiers on the streets of Fallujah. Clearly, this isn't about a missed turn signal. They think we're terrorists.

A cop with a crew cut shines his Maglite in each of our faces. He stops for a few extra seconds on me. Then he asks me to open the back half of the door. "No problem," I say, mentally crossing my fingers that the cooler doesn't spill. I swing open the door, and somehow, miraculously, the Igloo stays upright. But it's right there in the flashlight beam, hiding in plain sight.

Crew Cut brings the light back to my face and says, "Can I see your identification please?"

"Just mine?" I say.

"Just yours." He looks from my driver's license photo to my face three times. Then he disappears into the darkness.

The commando-cops keep working the van with their flashlights. Veins throb in their foreheads. I have to remind myself to breathe.

Long minutes later, Crew Cut returns. "You guys a band or something?"

"We're playing the Local 506 tonight," I say, referring to the club that has booked us.

"That's an alright place," he says, leaning in and shining a beam through the van once more. Then he straightens up. Takes a step back. "Look, fellas, here's the deal. We're tracking an escaped convict. A cop killer. And word comes over the wire that this asshole and his old lady are driving a van something like yours here." He drums his fingers on the roof. "We've been watching you all night."

The way he's staring holes through me, it's clear that by "watching you," he means watching *me*.

"When I was walking the Red Roof lot?" I ask. "Talking on the phone?"

"We had one team in the cruiser, and me and my guys were in the woods with binoculars." He gives a half-smile and looks down to the beer cooler and back. "Happy birthday."

I wonder if his guys intercepted my conversations, if they heard all the things husbands and wives say when they're five-hundred miles apart. Do they know Pooch is hours from fatherhood? Do they know that my nephews' lungs and eyes have yet to develop?

He gives my license a final once-over, and a little whistle escapes his lips. "I'll be dammed if you don't look *exactly* like the escapee," he says, handing me my ID. "I mean, just like him."

August 10, 2005. Columbus, OH.

George and Jennifer Hyatte are not laying low at the Durham Red Roof. They're holed up in the America's Best Value Inn on Sinclair Road in my hometown. As I'm being mistaken for George by the Chapel Hill PD, the two fugitives are hiding just across the railroad tracks from my mom's house.

After shooting Cotton Morgan, the Hyattes dumped Jennifer's Explorer, stole a minivan, and sped north on I-75 toward Ohio. They stopped in the Cincinnati suburb of Florence, Kentucky, to buy a hacksaw at Lowe's, which they used to free George from the cuffs and shackles. Then they caught a few hours' sleep in the Florence Econo Lodge. Come morning they chucked Jennifer's Glock into the hotel dumpster, left the minivan outside their room, and paid a cab driver named Mike Wagers $200 to drive them to Columbus.

They checked into the Best Value on Wagers's recommendation. When the cabbie returned to Kentucky and heard mention on the news of the manhunt, he called the police.

And now officers storm into the Hyattes' hotel room. They pull George's t-shirt over his head to disorient him. They handcuff Jennifer, who keeps repeating, "Baby, it'll be okay." Even as the cops push George and Jennifer apart, she insists, "It'll be okay, baby. It'll be okay."

August 11, 2005. Durham, NC.

Morning at the Red Roof. I wake to a domestic dispute. Two voices out in the parking lot.

Bitch, I ain't standing for this shit no more.

Good. Don't fucking stand for it. Walk, motherfucker. Walk your ass for it.

I turn on the TV to drown out the shouting. A CNN reporter stands in a motel parking lot in Columbus: *In the Hyattes' room, police found uneaten burritos and empty soda cans and a receipt from Lowe's in the garbage. Bedding was strewn about the room, and the sheets were stained with what appeared to be blood.*

August 11, 2005. Columbus, OH.

Pooch's wife gives birth to a beautiful girl. Mother, daughter, and guitar player are healthy and happy.

August 11, 1969. Stoughton, WI.

As I sleep through my second day in the nursery, my mom celebrates her thirty-fourth birthday by dozing in a hospital bed. It was a long, tough delivery, and as the doctor told her, she's not as young as most first-time mothers.

My dad smokes cigarettes in the waiting room, letting his wife rest. He shakes open the morning paper, rubs his sideburns, and exhales. Scanning the columns, he's both stunned and not by the harm we visit upon each other. He was a priest. He's seen us at our best and worst, and even though he's reading what he's reading, he's betting that this world and those who inhabit it are redeemable. To believe otherwise is to quit living.

> *LOS ANGELES (AP)—Police pushed a manhunt today for a suspect in the bizarre killings of actress Sharon Tate and four others five miles from where a couple was found slain later in a similar style.*
>
> *"There is a similarity, but whether it's the same suspect or a copycat we just don't know," said Police Sgt. Bryce Houchin.*
>
> *At the scene of the second slayings, Inspector K. J. McCauley said, "I don't see any connection between this murder and the others. They're too widely removed. I just don't see any connection."*

August 11, 2005. Columbus, OH.

My mom turns seventy today. She pours herself a cup of Maxwell House and flips through the *Columbus Dispatch*. The cop-killing Hyattes captured. More U.S. soldiers and Iraqi civilians dead. She walks across her front lawn to the elm tree where she has built a make-do war memorial. For every American soldier who has died in Iraq and Afghanistan, she has placed a stone along the base of the tree. This morning she holds stone number two-thousand.

She spends the rest of her birthday between two incubators at Riverside. Her grandchildren are not much bigger than her open palm. She can see the veins pulsing beneath their translucent skin. Their skin is coarse and dry, not smooth as a baby's anything.

Four months later, I hang a poem on my refrigerator, written by my dad to his grandsons.

We vowed in their presence
No war
No death
No more
We will not send them
They are gifts
Not to be spoiled
Nor given back in any August

—2008

Two Haircuts

1. Home

The Ohio Barber and Beauty College. A two-story building in the satellite lot of Northland Mall. An Eisenhower-era crew cut in poured concrete and low-slung steel. Sterile and stern. Everything set at ninety degrees to everything else.

The temperature drops five degrees on the walk from our VW Rabbit to the entrance. Holding the door open for my mom and little sister, Jill, I smell the ammonia of the hair dye and the musky Wella Balsam conditioner and the alcohol solution that disinfects the scissors. If the veterinarian's office smells anything like this to our dog Rex, I understand why she pulls so hard against the leash.

I'm fourteen and hyper-aware of my body and the various tufts and patches that cover it. I tirelessly monitor my hair, measuring its response to wind and wool sweaters and my Milwaukee Brewers cap. I can't walk past a parked car without checking my reflection in the windows.

My mom is at the counter talking to a man in a lab coat and army-issue glasses. Jill and I are sitting on the vinyl waiting area couch, flipping through year-old copies of *People* and *Life*. On the coffee table is a glossy book that looks like a magazine but is really a hundred pages of glamour shots compiled by some beauty product company. Six models with six different hairstyles on every page. They look like the most style-forward senior class in high school history. The Alberto VO5 class of 1984.

"So, did you find the one you want?" the woman asks me. She's got smoky blonde hair, moussed into submission. A few loose strands are stuck to the v-neck and shoulders of her pea-green smock. Her makeup is too thick: her blush too red, her shadow too blue. The fluorescent lighting gives away the scars from a bout with acne.

I reach from the sample hairstyle book to my own pimpled chin. "Huh?"

"Did you find the *style* you want, hon?" She takes my hand. My legs make a sucking sound as I rise from the couch.

What do I want? I want to be Tom Cruise in *Risky Business*. I want the Ray-Ban Wayfarers and the Porsche 928. I want to have sex with Rebecca DeMornay on a fast moving L-train.

She walks me back toward two long rows of barber chairs. Sitting in each chair is a wiry guy who looks like a truck driver, his vein- and tattoo-laced forearms locked stiff on the arm rests. Or a fat lady in Chic jeans bursting with phlegmy laughter. Or a soda-straw-skinny kid with off-brand tennis shoes and in desperate need of broccoli. Circling each chair, scissors snipping away, is a student barber in a pea-green smock. They're all wearing docksiders or black high-top Reeboks, and they step through piles of clipped hair. A few serious, lab-coated men and women pace from chair to chair, offering instruction or muted praise. A bent-over black guy pushes a broom across the floor.

As she dips my head back into the u-shaped groove cut into the sink, I stare up at the ceiling tiles. There are a thousand little pencil holes poked into each white square. The night sky in negative. She massages the shampoo through my hair, her charm bracelets clinking against my forehead as she works her way around my scalp. Her fingernails are moving in expanding and collapsing circles. I've forgotten how good it feels to have someone wash your hair. She guides the water from the spray nozzle away from my eyes, pushing it back over the top of my head. She reaches for the conditioner, and I catch a whiff of her perfume. She's right over me, blocking out whole galaxies in ceiling tile. I look down the v-neck of her smock and see a full inch of lace. I'm getting hard under my gym shorts. I'm suddenly thankful for the apron I'm wearing.

She straightens to open the bottle. "Look," she says, taking up small sections of wet hair and smoothing them between her fingers. "You've already got a receding hairline."

"Yeah," I say. But I don't know what she means.

2. Away

Kate and I are in Kusadasi, Turkey, on our honeymoon. We're strolling through narrow streets, shaking our heads as politely as we can at the carpet salesmen and their offers of apple tea and lessons in the finer points of Oriental rug making. This is early May, the low season. There's no behemoth cruise ship in port to make the bright little fishing skiffs look like bathtub boats. We see no other tourists in this tourist-town.

At the fringe of a bazaar where wrinkled women sell evil eyes and bootleg Calvin Klein underwear, we come to a barbershop. The barber himself is the only person inside. He's sitting in his own chair. Seeing us, he hops up and gestures for me to take a seat in that red naugahyde contraption, so similar to the ones in which, as a balding teenager, I spent a hundred uncomfortable Saturdays.

I've been shaving my head skin-bald for six years—ever since the morning of my twenty-fourth birthday when I first took a dollop of Barbasol and a single-blade Bic to my disloyal scalp. Not knowing how to say anything in Turkish other than *thank you* and *good night*, I point to my stubbled head and make a palms-up, what-are-you-gonna-do shrug. The barber laughs and with mock forcefulness takes my elbow, leading me into the shop. I turn that same resigned shrug toward Kate and climb into the chair, thinking, *This is the set-up to a bad joke. "So a bald guy walks into a barbershop..."*

First he rubs my head and face with lotion that smells strongly of sage. He massages my skull and kneads the cords that run the back of my neck. He pushes his thumbs deep between my shoulder blades. He grips my shoulders and slides his grip down my arms, which now feel an inch longer. Then he squeezes a dab of cream into his palm and presses his hands together for several seconds to warm it.

The shop is florescent orange and immaculate. It smells like lemons. We don't say anything, the barber and I. We *can't* say anything. Instead, we exchange an occasional roll of the eye or up-tick of the mouth. We point and nod. And I'm at home in the hands of this Turkish stranger.

He smoothes the shaving cream over my head and under my cheekbones. Then, breaking into a smile, he pulls out a four-inch straight razor. In the mirror, I can see Kate holding her breath. The barber sees it, too. He turns and gestures in a way that says not to worry; he's a professional.

He squints, concentrating on the razor. After each pass, he swipes the blade clean with a freshly laundered towel. The high carbon steel makes a pleasant scraping sound as it erases twelve hours of stubble. Soon there are only a few streaks of shaving cream left on my head. He wipes those away with another towel and motions for me to feel how slick my scalp is. I know I'll never have a closer shave.

I'm smiling at Kate in the mirror when a blue flame appears in my peripheral vision. Kate's eyes grow wide and worried. So do mine. The barber has taken a long cotton swab, dipped it in alcohol, and lit it on fire. He cups my shoulder to hold me steady as he swoops the burning swab past my ears, singeing the baby hair from the outer folds. He moves to the other ear and then goes to work under my nose. Except for my eyebrows, not a single hair escapes.

He finishes by rubbing a blend of alcohol and lemon oil into my scalp, my cheeks, my neck. Then he claps his hands as if to say,

Voila! He's a proud man. He takes his craft seriously. As Kate pays him, he nods and says what must be the only English he knows, "Okay. Bye."

I shake his hand and say everything I know to say. "Teşekkür ederim. Iyi aksamlar." *Thank you. Good night.*

—2007

II. AMERICAN INTERIORS

This Essay Doesn't Rock

You may be tempted to argue otherwise. After all, this is an essay concerning sex, drugs, and rock 'n' roll—that archetypal trinity of a certain kind of "rocking" lifestyle. But the mere appearance of these three classic indicators of rock does not a rocking essay make. In fact, *rocking essay* is an oxymoron. Essaying—the crafted attempt to weigh an issue in order to gain a deeper understanding of it—by definition does not rock. I say this not because I have access to a specific definition of what rock *is*, but instead because I think I have a pretty clear sense of what rock *is not*. Rock is not crafted. Rock is not calculated. Rock is not honed and edited and revised. It is not logical or cohesive or polite—at least it shouldn't be. Rock is not trying to get you to think. Rock doesn't care what you think. And although rock may be heavy, it certainly doesn't *weigh* anything, at least not anything that approaches significant societal import. (It often does, however, weigh the relative merits of rock itself, e.g., whether one should or should not rock—or be rocked—longer or harder or louder or like a hurricane.)

Rock is a slippery concept, subject to varied and contradictory interpretations. To my grandparents' generation, *rock* is what one does in an unfinished wooden chair U-hauled home from Amish Country. Before they got old, baby boomers used the verb *to rock* to mean "playing rock 'n' roll music" or "living the rock 'n' roll life-style." The word, like the music itself, suggested urgency, shameless-

ness, a need to run counter to the suit-and-tie establishment, and a
general tendency to not give a good-goddamn about anything but
the here and now. But as rock music and its original audience have
aged, the word *rock* has aged with them. In 21st century America,
rock has been watered down to mean something benign like *a little
better than awesome* or *a slightly more ass-kickin' kick-ass*. In this
form, *rock* is less a verb and more a verbal—a verb doing the work
of an adjective.[1] *Rock/rocks* sits toward the far right on a continuum
of positive and negative modifiers.

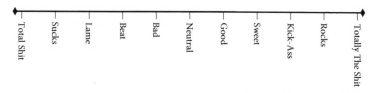

The opposite of *rocks* is *sucks*. And to be blunt, the current usage
of *rocks* does just that. The word has been commandeered by advertising agencies, cheerleading squads, and other sloganeering types
who assault us with an endless list of things that rock. We are told:
*Fruity Pebbles Rock! Westerville North Girls Volleyball Rocks! The
Coast Guard Rocks! The Fourth Avenue Peace Coalition Rocks! We
Rock! You Rock! Doesn't This All Just Totally Rock?* No. It doesn't. But
I'm not being entirely fair here. _____ *Rocks!* is not strictly the
domain of pitchmen, political operatives, and high school hallway
decorators. Even supposed rockers are guilty of this assault on the
word.[2] I'd like to think the twenty years I've spent playing bass and
singing in a band have taught me a little something about what rocks
and what doesn't. And still, I find myself getting sloppy and saying

---

1. Come to think of it, most of the corporate, stylized, focus-group-approved
muck that currently passes for rock music is also more adjective than verb—a
dressed-up modifier of something that once rocked rather than actual rocking.
2. In fact, most of us in bands are the last to know what rocks, hence the pitch-
perfect film *This Is Spinal Tap*.

ridiculous crap like "Ohio State's defense rocks!" all the time. But this corruption has got to stop. Because if *Ms. Mulcahy's third graders rock*, then everything rocks. And if everything rocks, nothing rocks.

Saying something rocks has become an accepted way to describe things that patently do not rock, but even more ironically, the word is often used to prop up and make credible the same straight-laced, establishment-approved things that rock and roll used to rally against. This became clear to me during the 2004 Republican National Convention. Our burly codger of a Vice President saddled up to the podium with a half wave and a crooked grin, and the camera cut to the conventioneers on the floor. Right there, in the sea of *Bush-Cheney '04* signs, floating above the chants of *Four More Years!*, on a poster board with block letters that must have taken three or four Sharpies to fill in, it said:

DICK CHENEY ROCKS!!![3]

Now, look. Dick Cheney is obviously a man of power and influence. He served in the Nixon White House. He was a five-term congressman. House Minority Whip. He led the charge to invade Iraq. He's got a seat in the Situation Room. But Dick Cheney does not rock. Whatever you think of him as a man and a politician, surely we can agree on this point. I know, I know. The Republicans want to be the party of inclusiveness. They call themselves coalition builders. They're constructing a big tent in which we can all feel welcome. But what would happen if an actual rock star like a Keith Moon circa '70 or a Keith Richards circa '77 or a strung-out Johnny Thunders circa '88 were to crash this metaphorical tent party? My guess is that Dick Cheney would be choppered out like at the fall of Saigon. Maybe this is an unfair scenario. The three above rockers all rock in a specific, old-fashioned, snorting-coke-off-the-mixing-board kind of way. But I know one thing: Dick Cheney and Keith

---

3. Punctuation in original. Exclamation points are a reliable indicator of non-rock. The more exclamation points, the less rock. Count on it.

Richards can't both rock. In order for *rock* to mean anything at all, we must choose.

But the choice isn't between a Republican and a Rolling Stone. That choice is obvious and pointless. Everyone knows Richards rocks, and sane people know Cheney doesn't. There's no universally agreed upon standard. We just know it. Intuitively. Much like Supreme Court Justice Potter Stewart stating that he couldn't provide a satisfactory definition of pornography but that he knew it when he saw it, most of us can recognize rock when we see, hear, smell, feel, or taste it.[4] Does Keith Richards rock? Christ, just look at him. Sixty-odd years of rock are carved into his face. He's a one-man Mount Rushmore of rock, the (somehow still) living, breathing template. And Cheney? Uh, no. Power lunches at The Palm on DuPont Circle aren't so much carved into his face as they are spilling over his shirt collar. Obviously the definition of *rock* can't be so wide as to include Cheney, but it can't be so narrow as to include only Keith. Just as *rock* probably can't embrace those who hold breakfast meetings with conservative Christian groups, it also can't be limited to those who've copped heroin in Tompkins Square.

So if we all have some DNA-level knowledge of what rock is, how did we get to the place where even the stuff we know *does not* rock is still filed under rock? Society writ-large was once both fascinated and repelled by rock and roll music and the antics of its practitioners. In 1969,[5] the year I was born, Jim Morrison—the bloated, ex-film student and self-coronated Lizard King[6]—exposed

---

4. What does rock taste like? Something like that mouthful of warm beer from a can that's been used as an ashtray. Unexpected.

5. Getting sophomoric laughs from the number 69 does not rock. However, I've noticed that the Ohio Department of Transportation has erected signs on every Interstate and US route that point out when you are exactly 69 miles from Columbus. Not 65. Not 70. Not 75. *Sixty-nine.* Giggle.

6. Giving yourself a nickname or acknowledging the nickname someone else has given you does not rock. But, strangely enough, a stage name (a *nom de guerre*, if you will) can rock. Rock is funny that way.

himself to a Miami audience. This got him arrested, charged, and eventually convicted of lewd and lascivious behavior, but it also helped to create the persona that would make Morrison a cultural icon, and it certainly made the Doors a more popular band. Would anyone today notice, much less *care*, if Billie Joe Armstrong from Green Day—that heavily eyelined father of two and singer for the current biggest band in the world—dropped his drawers on stage? I suppose a few minivan driving chaperones would write fiery letters to the daily paper, but it certainly wouldn't cause a Morrison-sized stink. And my guess is it wouldn't affect Green Day's popularity either way.

This is not because our view of what is lewd and lascivious has changed. (We still don't cotton to the free-swinging of male genitalia—the almost-guaranteed X-rating for a movie featuring a naked penis testifies to that.) Instead, it's our view of rock and roll (and rock and rollers) that has changed. Rock music has become so ubiquitous as to be invisible. As it moved from being a voice of the counterculture to being an integrated part of The Culture, it didn't exactly fall off the cultural radar, but it became so *on* the cultural radar that it is now the background noise that other, suddenly edgier cultural movements are made vivid against. Rock and roll is not any less dangerous or urgent than it ever was.[7] The difference is in how we perceive it. The fact is we no longer look to rock music to fulfill our need to rebel or be shocked. Instead, we are simultaneously shocked and fascinated by the "thug lifestyle" glorified by ex–drug dealing rappers. We worry that our kids will

---

7. It's true that years of mergers and acquisitions and the steady process of vertical and horizontal integration have reduced "the music business" to three multinational mega-corporations: Sony/Bertelsmann A.G., Time Warner, and Universal Music Group. Their need to answer to shareholders puts a governor on any real "danger" we might find in the music we hear on the radio or see topping the charts. There is, of course, plenty of rock and roll that remains infused with the immediacy that once said, "rock," but we have to look hard for it. "Little Steven's Underground Garage" on Sirius Satellite radio is a good place to start.

be contaminated by "gangsta rap" videos that make violence look sexy and sex look violent. We can't believe that our kids have access to bloody video games like the *Grand Theft Auto* series that allow them to virtually act out this sex and violence. And just like our own parents, and their parents before, we think back to a day when things were simpler: when kids liked baseball, people wished they could buy the world a Coke, and the biggest danger at a rock show was that the drunken lead singer might unzip his pants.

Rock music was rebellion, an act of defiance, a shaggy spit-in-the-face to Eisenhower's high and tight America. But as soon as the baby boomers seized control of America's institutions, they commodified rock and roll. Suddenly the music of Dylan and Janice Joplin and The Stones was being co-opted by ad executives and used to sell cars and computer software. Sex, drugs, and rock 'n' roll—the very weapons of the revolution—were used to market bourgeois luxuries to the same people that once rocked in rebellion against the bourgeoisie. Today, many of those formerly shaggy parents *encourage* their kids to form rock bands. It seems like once a year I read a story in the paper about a couple of freewheeling suburbanites who have outfitted their garage with a state of the art PA system, space-age soundproofing, and digital recording gear so little Hunter and his buddies in the cul-de-sac can have a place to, ahem, *rock out*. Forming a band is seen as a good, clean, parentally endorsed alternative to other types of rebellion...at least until Hunter comes home with a baggie of cocaine hidden in his amplifier. Yep, today everybody loves the rock—but only up to the point when it becomes dangerous, which is to say the point when rock truly *rocks*.

Again the problem is not that *rock* has lost its meaning but, rather, that it means too much. So maybe the current climate— in which anything somebody likes is said to "rock"—provides an opportunity to construct some standard to help us gauge who or what is truly rocking and how hard he, she, or it is doing it.[8] Of course, attempting to codify *rock* by applying a fixed set of qualifications is probably the least rocking thing I can imagine.[9] But anyway, here I go. Back to the beginning.

Sex, drugs, and rock 'n' roll.

That's the standard. And why not? The thinking has already been done for us. Three easy-to-remember categories. Like most things that obviously rock, the beauty lies in the simplicity. Cheerleaders and advertising executives won't even have to stop using the word to describe their wrestling team or F-150 trucks or whatever; they'll just have to be more judicious in its use. Before spelling out *Cardinal Wrestling Rocks!* in Elmer's Glue and glitter dust, the vernacularly responsible cheerleader will stop to consider how the wrestling team measures up in the three criteria. No sex? No drugs? No rock 'n' roll? Then no rocks.

But wait. As I mention above, the standard must be broad enough to be useful, and insisting on all three categories makes meeting them far too difficult for people who aren't in Mötley Crüe.[10] So I'll propose a compromise: two out of three. Sex and drugs. Rock and sex. Drugs and rock. This idea was inspired by Spinal Tap drummer Mick Shrimpton. In *This Is Spinal Tap*, when he's asked what he'd be doing if he weren't in a rock and roll band, he answers, "I suppose as long as I had the sex and drugs, I could do without the rock and roll." Leave it to the fictional drummer of a semifictional band to say something that captures the nature of rock perfectly. Mr. Shrimpton knows that with the sex and the drugs, the rock 'n' roll is superfluous. He wouldn't need it, because he'd already be rocking.

---

8. Rock is always measured in terms of hardness. Just like actual rocks.

9. Check that. The Rock and Roll Hall of Fame is the least rocking thing I can imagine. The self-sanctioned institutionalization of rock music may have been the death knell. That said, it's a fantastic museum, and I have a great time every time I visit.

10. The use of irönic *umlauts* and devil horn fists rocks when somebody who rocks does it. This is totally dependent on context.

The SDR&R standard (with the Shrimpton addendum) seems like a reasonable way to measure rockness, but let's apply it to a test case and see if it holds. I hope it goes without saying that Christian rock doesn't rock—that rocking for God, however righteous or commercially successful it may be, isn't really rocking. Two generations of rock journalists[11] have already established that the devil has the better musical acts in his corner. But still, for argument's sake, let's see how Christian rock measures up to the SDR&R standard. Take the last criterion, "rock 'n' roll." I could contend that Christian rock isn't even rock music, that rock and roll must contain some element of sex and drugs to even *be* rock and roll, but that would get dizzyingly circular. Instead, I'll concede that Christian rock, because the bands generally utilize the prototypical instrumentation (electric guitar, bass, drums), is in fact rock music. Besides, most Christian rock is indiscernible at first listen from what Christian rockers call "secular" rock, until the lyrics sink in and you make out the not-quite-veiled references to a loved one who could either be a lover or the Almighty or both. So, if it sounds like rock music, maybe it is, and one element out of three is nailed.[12] However, I'm afraid Christian rock's active stance against snorting drugs and having indiscriminate sex prevents it from meeting the SDR&R standard. Christian rock might be rock music, but it doesn't rock.

The very words *rock and roll* from their inception were a kind of code for sex; they even *sound* like sex—or at least a description of sex. And until fairly recently, rock music only endorsed (overtly, anyway) heterosexual sex. But this brings me to the first of two important caveats to the SDR&R standard: *Rock must continually confound our expectations.* For example, cycles of strict heterosexuality tend to lead

11. Christian rockers, take heart: Rock journalism doesn't rock either. But rock journal*ists* can rock. See Lester Bangs and Chuck Klosterman.

12. But this *sounds like rock* quality is exactly what has so many people confused. And their use of "secular" to describe everything that isn't Christian rock is a move meant to legitimize Christian rock itself. Christian rockers are very crafty.

to a kind of testosterone-fueled meat-headishness that simply does not rock.[13] This in turn creates a counter-movement toward sexual ambiguity and at least a token acknowledgment of homosexuality. And this confounds our expectations. Listening to the rock and roll canon, we might expect heterosexual sex to rock harder than homosexual sex, but this is not a sure bet. In a climate of prevailing heterosexuality, homosexuality rocks harder. But as soon as this homosexuality plays like a blatant and conscious attempt to be perceived as rock (and sell a bunch of records), it doesn't rock at all.[14]

This brings me to caveat number two: *As soon as something self-identifies as "rocking"; as soon as it becomes conscious of its own attempt to rock; as soon as it too obviously tries to convince you that it does rock, it almost certainly does not, regardless of the amount of sex or drugs or rock 'n' roll.*

A few years ago, I stopped by my friend Phil's guitar shop to buy a few packs of bass strings. As I reached into the rack to pull out my old standbys, I noticed a new product from the GHS string company called "Nickel Rockers"—*Nickel*, as in the metal the strings are made of, and *Rockers*, as in either these strings rock or guitarists who play these strings will rock. Phil has been playing, fixing, and selling guitars for a long time, and I've come to him often for advice, but while paying for my strings, my question to him was this: "Hey Phil, what kind of self-respecting 'rocker' would ever buy strings called 'Nickel Rockers?'"

"I don't know," he said. "It's stupid."

"But here's the thing," I said, handing him my credit card. And I paused for a second because I knew I was about to use a word that is

13. See Limp Bizkit. This *engorged penis rock* also confuses people. It sounds like rock, and it is irrefutably "hard." But it is far too predictable and *unsexy* to truly rock. Can you imagine having sex with someone who fucks like this music sounds?

14. This is why Russian lesbian duo t.A.t.U do not rock, but Canadian lesbian (twin sister) duo Tegan and Sara do.

just about as offensive and hurtful as it gets in my circles. "If these strings were called GHS Nickel Faggots, then I would buy them in a second."

"Yeah, it's funny," he said. "'Rockers' is gay, but 'faggots' rocks."

Here we see much of what is true and infuriating and confusing about rock. In this single statement, we get the notion that (a) rock is contradictory; (b) it undermines our expectations; (c) it shouldn't be too blatant in announcing itself as rock; and (d) as soon as it leans too hard in one direction, it must reverse itself. Perhaps the most frustrating contradiction is that even as rock appears to make room for homosexuality (by conceding that "'faggots' rocks"), this seeming empowerment is then undermined by the use of "gay" to signify the worst kind of not-rocking.

But here's the ultimate problem with trying to apply standards—be they my requirement for sex and drugs and rock 'n' roll or the 1950s-style standards of decency—to what rocks. Let's say I could get everyone to agree to my SDR&R standard, with the Shrimpton addendum and the two caveats, and everyone from you and me to *Extra's* Dayna Devon only used *rock* in reference to people and things that meet the standard. (*Keith Richards rocks, a meth-fueled blowjob in a bathroom stall rocks*, etc.) As soon as that was achieved, one ornery upsetter—maybe even little Hunter from the cul-de-sac—would surely decide that all of us, with our guitars and amps, and our sex and drugs, and our ex-hippie parents, and our standards and addendums and caveats were one-hundred-percent full of shit, and what really rocks, what *really, really* rocks is *Project Runway* or Rachel Ray or, hell, maybe even Christian rock. And you know what? He'd have a point.

Once we'd measured precisely what rocks, there would be, as Sammy Hagar tells us, only one way to rock. And that way would be to do a one-eighty against everyone else. Hunter would rock by trading his guitar for a three-piece suit, by quitting his garage band

and joining the debate and forensic team. He'd rock by becoming an actuary for an insurance company. Or maybe he'd go into politics instead. Why mess around? The hardest rockers would step right up and join the establishment. He'd become a five-term congressman, get a job in the White House, arrange breakfast meetings with conservative Christians.

So maybe Dick Cheney does rock.

Power and wealth are sexy. I mean, chicks dig rich, powerful guys, right? So, there's the sex. And America's presence in Afghanistan gives us access to most of the world's supply of the opium poppy. There's the drugs. Now the Veep has two out of three. But maybe he doesn't even need the sex, drugs, and rock 'n' roll. What if, despite my adherence to the SDR&R standard, the one true criterion for rock is simply the ability to convince somebody that you *do* rock. I suppose if Cheney can somehow motivate somebody, anybody—even a Republican delegate—to break open a package of Sharpies and spring for $.79 worth of poster board with which to declare his rockingness for all the world to behold, then goddamn it. All I can say is rock on, Mr. Vice President. Rock on.

—2006

The Botch Job

I've got a bad tattoo, bad because it represents the flawed execution of an ill-conceived idea. The idea was bad for the usual reasons: I was young, rash, insecure; my aesthetic sense was half-formed at best. How bad is the execution? On a scale of one to ten, with one being "Stabbed in the Chest with a Bic" and ten "The Tattoo Equivalent of Michelangelo's *The Creation of Adam*," I'd say mine clocks in at about a four ("Drunken Hackery")—which is obviously better than two ("Rusty Sewing Needle in Juvie") and three ("Right-Handed Artist Experiments with Left Hand"), but still it's not a feature I'm proud to show off. The tattoo is inked to the meat of my left shoulder, where most of the time it's hidden from public view, but roll my sleeve all the way up, and you'll see a hazy blue apparition that once read *Wallflower Child*, the title of a song I wrote. It's been twenty-three years since I went under the gun; the color has faded past mute, and the letters have melted to illegibility. Take a greasy White Castle box and let it bake on your dashboard for six months—that's a fair approximation of the tattoo I've got.

As far as I know, there's no easy way to un-get it. A quick Internet search tells me that removal treatments not only don't work but are also usually more expensive and painful than the original tattoo, so a better option is to cover up the old image with a new one. But that seems like throwing good money after bad. Besides, now that the fog of my youth has lifted and I'm a forty-five-year-old English professor and father of two, I can't think of a single image so meaningful that I'd voluntarily wear it for the second half of my life. *Palimpsest* would be the most logical (and literal) choice, but nobody other than my colleagues in the English department would get the joke. Plus, the risk of misspelling seems awfully high. *Palinfest? Ballincest?*

Since I can't think of one image I'd want, maybe I should take the advice of Ilona, a professional tattoo artist, who, in a blog post entitled "7 Steps to Successful Tattoo," lists Step #1 as KNOW WHAT YOU DO NOT WANT!

Shoot, Ilona, that's easy. I do not want a scorpion. I do not want a lion. I do not want a red devil or a grim reaper. No Mexican skulls. No Celtic knots. Definitely no barbed wire. No great white sharks or Japanese carp. No Chinese characters or Native American tribal bands—nothing whose meaning I'd have to look up. I do not want a Yosemite Sam. I do not want green eggs and ham. I do not want an anchor, although I've got to admit that the anchor (like the nautical star and the classic "Mom"-in-a-heart) holds an old school, salty dog appeal—but it wouldn't really count unless I got it done in Singapore (and, better yet, during a stint with the Merchant Marine) or in Shanghai (and then only if I'd actually been shanghaied). I do not want an American flag or a bald eagle or Lady Liberty. I do not want the Nike swoosh or the Apple apple. No barcodes and no QR codes, even though I feel just as homogenized and commoditized by this hegemonic superstructure as everyone else.

I can see how in the face of so much capitalistic conformity, a new tattoo might be one way to stake out my fierce individuality. I could go with *Unique* or *Enigma* or some other word that captures me in all my complex *me*-ness. *Ambivalent*, maybe. But I do not want to think that I'm so simple a creature that my identity can be reduced to a single word. I do not want an outward manifestation of my internal belief system. I do not want to broadcast what I most value via a medium that's been cheapened by its very ubiquity.

Turns out, I know exactly what I do not want. I do not want a tattoo. That's the whole point.

***

My, ahem, *work*, as a professional tattoo artist like Ilona might call it, was not, in fact, done by a professional tattoo artist but, rather, by a buddy of mine, John Speck, a guitar player/skateboarder who dabbled in tattooing the way my wife now experiments with homemade ricotta. This was in Detroit, in 1991, late on a Sunday morning. Speck and I were nursing hangovers in the basement of a house on Eight Mile Road that he shared with the guys in his band, The Generals. As I sat fidgeting in a folding chair, he was assembling the tattoo gun. The night before Watershed had driven up to Michigan from Columbus to do a show with The Generals. My bandmates and I had recently dropped out of Ohio State, where I'd been an honor student, and climbed into a beat-up van, trying to carve out a future that wouldn't be lived in an office cubicle. We'd played shows in Louisville and Indy, Toledo and Milwaukee. Now we were in Detroit, where houses had bars on the windows and guitarists kept tattoo guns in their backpacks. With its crumbling buildings and vacant lots, Detroit might as well have been Beirut or Bosnia. And to me, a twenty-two-year-old son of the suburbs, it was the coolest place on the planet.

As we loaded the gear out of the bar, I tried to read the tattoos on Speck's forearm, but there were so many, it was hard to separate one from the next. He was only nineteen, and he already had a full sleeve. Ninety-percent coverage, easy. I'd never seen such high tattoo density. I thought tattoos were still the exclusive domain of bikers and longshoremen, juvenile delinquents and mechanics. Back in Columbus, I knew only one guy with a tattoo, a guy named Dave Cook, and he was, in fact, a juvenile delinquent mechanic who rode a motorcycle, and he would have made a hell of a longshoreman had he not lived more than a hundred miles from the nearest shore. None of my fellow Poli Sci majors had been tattooed. Neither had most of the musicians Watershed had played with since we dropped out of college. To me, Speck *was* an enigma. But it wasn't just Speck. Everyone in Detroit seemed tatted up, which obviously speaks to my suburban college-boy perspective, but that's precisely the point. In 1991, tattoos weren't yet mainstream—except in Detroit, where, along with nipple piercings, chain wallets, platform creeper shoes, and all the other rocking accoutrements that ten years later would be found on sixteen-year-old mall rats from Poughkeepsie to Peoria, they were just a regular part of the day-to-day.

By the time we got to The Generals' house for the after show party, I'd decided to ask Speck to give me one. Right then. I knew I was being reckless, but I didn't care. Dropping out of school had been reckless, too, but I was happier than I'd ever been. My buddies and me, driving around the country, chasing a life different from the accounting and insurance adjusting jobs our classmates were headed for. We wanted nothing more than to make this time of our lives permanent.

"I can't tattoo you tonight," Speck said. "You're too drunk. You'll bleed like a stuck pig."

Bloody or not, I wanted to do it immediately, while I was too hammered to sweat the pain, before I could second-guess myself.

Speck shook his head.

"But wait," I said, and I tried to sell him on my idea: *Wallflower Child*, a song I'd written shortly after quitting school. I told him how this tune—about a shy kid who was finally coming into bloom— marked the perfect transition between my old self (school-bound and straitlaced) and the new version of me that was taking shape night by night in dive bars and dank basements.

"Rad," he said, "but sleep on it." He pointed to his full sleeve. "This is forever."

When I woke up, I was still drunk and still dead set on the tattoo. No retreat, baby. And like the title favorite of my Springsteen song, no surrender.

No Surrender might have made for a great tattoo design, but I was sold on *Wallflower Child*. Down in the basement, Speck took out a sheet of wax paper and worked up a quick sketch.

"Fuck yeah," I said. "Do it."

The gun buzzing like a hornet, Speck dug into my shoulder. I glanced down at the first streaks of blue *W* and held tight to the seat of the chair. I wasn't girding up against the pain so much as the perpetuity. As gung ho as I was, I knew I might one day regret having to wear *Wallflower Child* for the rest of my life. Maybe I should have given Speck's mock-up more than five seconds' consideration. Maybe I should have waited a few weeks until Watershed's next gig in Detroit, which would have given me time to take recommendations for actual tattoo artists. I could have paged through samples, seen photographic evidence of the artists' experience and skill. What was another week or three, compared to the permanence of a lifetime?

As Speck went about the business of laying the ink and wiping the blood, I told myself that the design didn't matter. Neither did the quality of the work. What mattered was the message, the words and what they represented: I was growing into the life my bandmates and I had dreamed for ourselves. And that, I knew, I'd never regret.

***

Epiphanies are all well and good, but they're fleeting. When I stand at the bathroom mirror now, I don't see the epiphany. I don't see "revelation" or "insight" or some other lofty abstraction. I see the tangible botched results. That's what lasts.

Maybe the best-case scenario would have been if Speck, unbeknownst to me, had used some sort of magic ink that disappeared after five years. That way, I could have congratulated myself for having the guts to commit to permanence without having to live with the visual consequence of that commitment. But obviously the only reason the rite of getting a tattoo holds any significance is because we know it will last forever. If tattoos weren't for life, they wouldn't matter. What gives a tattoo meaning is having to live down your decision to get it.

As bad as my tattoo is, I don't regret it, per se. I'm not sorry I chose *Wallflower Child*, and I'm actually kind of glad I asked Speck (an amateur, sure, but also a good friend and fellow lifer musician) to do it. It's just that I'm getting tired of looking at the dang thing. Most days, I guess, I don't really see it, any more than I see the little dipper of freckles on my chest or the scar that runs parallel to my left eyebrow or that copy of Rush's *Caress of Steel* that's been stuck in a CD binder, untouched for so long that the art has transferred from the disc to the plastic sleeve. Own anything long enough, and it becomes invisible. I'm only consciously aware of the tattoo when I'm at the pool or the beach, under the gaze of shirtless others, wondering what a smudgy, illegible *Wallflower Child* looks like to them and what they think it says about me—just as I'm only aware of *Caress of Steel* when somebody else flips through my CD collection.

I now teach college near Myrtle Beach, not far from the sand. At the beach and on campus, I see a heck of a lot of skin, and I can report that a goodly portion of South Carolina's epidermal real estate has been claimed by tattoos—on everyone from sorority girls to administrative assistants to marine biologists. Many of them surely cling to the fundamental tenet of body modification, that *the body is the canvas*. And I say more power to 'em. People should be free to decorate their bodies however they see fit. I'm starting to think, however, that the body isn't the canvas. The body's the *art*, and it's already a masterpiece. Nailing a tattoo on top of something that's perfect to begin with seems as silly as Sharpie-ing a smiley face over Picasso's "The Old Guitarist."

But, of course, even a silly act can be meaningful. Down in that Detroit basement, getting tattooed by a young guitarist, I thought *Wallflower Child*—the actual words—held the significance. Now that the tattoo is essentially unreadable, I understand that the words themselves don't really matter. If Speck had given me an X or a squiggly line, the tattoo would still mean what it means, because the significance of a tattoo isn't contained in the design. It isn't about the art, after all. Tattoos have always been more process than product. What a tattoo represents first and foremost is the decision to do it. The guts to go through with it. A tattoo is nothing more or less than a souvenir that marks the occasion of getting the tattoo.

So, yeah. I've got a bad tattoo, a botch job. And the only option is to wear it with something like pride.

—*2014*

Barreling into Uncool

Some men like to watch their wives having sex with other men. I'm not one of them. At least, I don't think I am.

On the "alternative lifestyles" website alt.com, a search of my zip code yields 1,301 male/female couples seeking men to join them for "casual encounters," "special relationships," and "a little playing around." In the Nerve.com personals, Irisheyes999 posts that he is content to "watch and learn." A husband and wife in their thirties with the handle Steffalump assure us, "There's a payoff for him in it too." I'm not exactly sure what this payoff might be, but I do know I'm not burning for a Friday night spent watching a stranger take Kate to a previously unscaled height of ecstasy. Still, another man recently helped me rekindle a love affair of sorts, and like Irisheyes, I watched. And I learned.

Kate and I were throwing a party for our Ohio State grad school friends, and as I rifled through my CD collection, I couldn't find a single album deserving a spot in the five-disc changer. Every record I owned seemed uncool, outdated, or moderately-cool-but-way-too-obvious. I played a safety and loaded the player with The Clash's *London Calling, Exile on Main Street* by the Stones, Elliott Smith's first record, and albums by Wilco and The Replacements. These were predictable, grad school-approved waters, and I felt like a coward for selecting the very tunes one would find on the jukebox of a standard college town dive bar. As the guests arrived, and the pile of coats on our bed grew, I was underwhelmed by the CDs I'd chosen and worried someone might stumble upon the stinkers I hadn't. *Lick It Up* by Kiss? Night Ranger's *Seven Wishes?* The entire Foghat catalog? I couldn't subject a townhouse full of folks fluent in narratology and semiotics to the eight-minute live version of "Fool For The City."

Then I saw Aaron flipping through my jewel cases, and my palms started to sweat. He was a PhD student in literature, a hipster from Omaha, the city, according to the *Times*, that was the current capital of hipsterdom. He wore Beatle boots, tailored blazers, and fitted dress shirts. His hair was strategically disheveled, and he was married to Jill, a six-foot, straw-haired siren of the Great Plains. I was about to be outed as shamefully uncool.

But Aaron made his hands into twin devil horns and barreled straight into uncool. Judas Priest. *Screaming For Vengeance.* I'd forgotten I even owned the album. I hadn't listened to it since I was a junior in high school. Back then the closest I'd come to a date was one awkward, truth-or-dare minute in a closet with a cute cheerleader named Lori.

As Aaron dropped the CD in the tray, I could make out snippets of a conversation, something about a Foucauldian reading of *David Copperfield.* Then with a majestic kick-drum and cymbal crash, K.K. Downing and Glenn Tipton's Flying V guitars sliced in harmony through the cocktail chatter. Aaron looked over at me and nodded. A few Victorianists laughed and stuck out their tongues, pretending to bang their heads. I wanted to leap for the stop button. But watching Aaron play air guitar, I just couldn't. He curled his lip, titled his head back, and moved into the spread-legged stance of a rock god.

"The Hellion" gave way to "Electric Eye," and Rob Halford's vocals growled from my speakers. Suddenly I was no longer in my living room, surrounded by my fellow grad students. The Two-Buck-Chuck, the Carr's water crackers, the baked brie—it had all disappeared. It was now 1983, and I was in eighth grade, standing on the gym floor at the middle school dance, armed with my own Flying V air-guitar, not knowing or caring if I'd ever get to kiss Lori in plain sight. I was hearing the melodic whine of Judas Priest for the first time. And I was loving it.

The world was now Aaron, a few hundred CDs, and me. Aaron worked my collection like a Turkish masseur. Music was reborn in his hands. He moved to "In The Dark" by Billy Squier. "Spirit of '76" by The Alarm. Tom Petty's "Change Of Heart." These were songs I had once loved but had long stopped hearing. Songs that when I was younger had opened in me whatever I had that might pass for chakras.

As AC/DC erupted through the living room, I was thirteen again, standing on a chair at my first rock concert, trying to see the stage from Row EE. But with this memory came the doubt and insecurity of a thirteen-year-old, because suddenly I was at the middle school again—this time outside on the kickball concrete, watching Lori get felt up by a wiry eighth grader with a moustache and a *Back in Black* t-shirt.

This got me thinking about how all relationships contain the threat of betrayal. Was Aaron, my personal DJ, rocking *with* me or *despite* me? Was he enraptured by the musical gems he'd unearthed? Or would he and Jill, the willowy Nebraskan, stagger home laughing at my lame CD collection?

My throat had gone dry with vulnerability when, from my speakers, Malcolm and Angus Young choked down on their guitar strings, Phil Rudd rode his booming floor-tom, Bon Scott let out an orgasmic little *ah-oh,* and AC/DC exploded into the chorus of "Highway To Hell." I belted the words out loud, and Aaron shot a wholly unironic, Joe Louis-caliber fist toward the ceiling.

If that fist is any indication, Aaron got something out of the arrangement. He had his way with my CDs without any emotional involvement. He mined the depths of my collection without compromising his hipster status, because for him there was no ownership. No commitment. It was just a casual encounter.

But like Mister Steffalump, there was a payoff for me, too. The act of Aaron playing my CDs *for* me reminded me that my relationship with music is built on a foundation of shared experience that transcends the songs themselves. My favorite songs can't be reduced to a clever guitar riff or two bars of heart-shattering vocal melody any more than Kate can be explained in the knuckles of her spine or the two dimples in her lower back. But it's important to stop and acknowledge these small, precious things, because these are the things that so often pull us into the long lasting and the transcendent. And they ultimately keep us there. Sometimes it takes another person to steer us toward what we already know.

In the end, it doesn't matter what Aaron thought of my albums. His enjoyment or lack thereof is immaterial. He was the other man, performing a service. His usefulness was derived solely by what he could teach me about my own music collection. He taught well. My CDs and I thank him.

And we're available Friday night if he's free.

—2008

The Upside Addiction

I backed into writing late, deciding at age thirty-five to apply to Ohio State's MFA in Creative Writing Program. Like many people on the downslope to forty, I'd found myself stuck in a career crisis, working all day at a job I hated (researching medical equipment) in order to afford nights and weekends spent doing what I loved (playing in a band). A graduate diploma in creative writing, I hoped, would lead to a more tolerable nine-to-five gig. But I knew my application was like a desperate Hail Mary pass. The odds of getting accepted into the program seemed perilously close to zero, not because I was old but because I hadn't yet written anything. I'd done term papers as a Political Science undergrad, of course, a degree that had taken me fourteen years to complete, and I'd spat out a few half-assed journal entries. I'd written songs, too. A whole bunch of songs. But no stories. No poems. No personal essays, either—which was a problem, since I was applying to OSU to study creative nonfiction, and until a month or so before I began the application process, I hadn't written a single piece of nonfiction that could even remotely be called creative.

I did have one thing going for me: I had life experience. Which is to say, I had material. I'd spent the previous twenty years playing bass and singing in Watershed, the band my high school buddies and I started the summer we turned fifteen. We stayed together post-graduation and through three years of college, and then, just before our senior year, we quit school to hit the road full time. We were exactly young and naïve enough to be convinced we'd score a fat record contract. And after three years of playing everywhere from Boston to Austin and building a nice following in Columbus—well, we did.

Epic Records signed us to a six-figure deal, and we moved to New York to start work on our major label debut. This was the big leagues. Our manager also represented The Fugees. Our A&R man was the guy who'd signed the platinum-selling Spin Doctors. Jim Steinman, the songwriter behind Meat Loaf, was producing our album, and the lead single from that record soon caught fire on Chicago's top-rated rock station, which led to more radio adds across the Midwest. We drew a crowd of nearly 10,000 to a show in Columbus, and the Epic brass hinted that the label would be sending us out on a summer tour of radio station festivals. We were twenty-five and on the launch pad to rock stardom.

I'll go ahead now and state the obvious: Rock stardom didn't happen. The reasons are many and complex, but I'll boil them down to one: The promotional resources of even a huge label like Epic are finite. Just as momentum was building for Watershed inside the company machine, label reps started showing up at our gigs asking if we'd heard about their newest signing, Silverchair, a group of teenagers from Australia. We hadn't—not at first, anyway—and when we told the reps as much, they always, and I mean *always*, said, "Those guys are really good…for sixteen-year-olds." That qualification ("for sixteen-year-olds") infuriated us. Watershed had already been together for ten years. The summer we'd formed the band, those Australian whippersnappers were still being carried in their mamas' kangaroo pouches. We were all twenty-five, nine years older than the Silverchair kids, but still, it's not like we were old, even by the music industry's skewed standards. Besides, the success of our single in Chicago was proof that our songs were viable regardless of our age.

No matter. When the Epic execs met to decide which band to put on the radio festival tour, they chose Silverchair. Then they dropped us from the label. Our big-shot manager, now busy representing Joan Osborne and Spacehog, called to tell us we'd had a nice run, but it was over.

If you'd asked me at the time, I would have said that choosing sixteen-year-olds over twenty-five-year-olds was another in a long line of examples of our culture's obsession with youth. But now—at forty-three, a more appropriate age from which to gripe about how we favor the young—I'm not entirely sure we *are* youth-obsessed. Instead, we seem to be intoxicated by *potential* and its riskier side-kick, *upside.*

The words *potential* and *upside* are almost, but not quite, synonymous. Both deal in possibility. Both are a bet on the future. But *potential* is the safer play, one that treats past performance as a predictor of future success. *Upside*, because it insinuates its opposite, *downside*, is the high-risk proposition—longer odds but a richer payoff. You'll see this dynamic at work every year during the NCAA basketball tournament, when talk inevitably turns to which players have the talent and skill to make the leap to the NBA. Many athletes—especially the freshmen who are projected to leave college after one year, the "one-and-dones"—are described in terms of their upside. Come draft day, the conservative pick will be the seasoned upperclassman, the known quantity, the one with mappable potential. But, oh, how teams will be tempted to go all-in on the raw-but-freakishly-gifted freshman, the bigger gamble with the unknowable (and therefore more enticing) upside.

Our addiction to upside is no surprise. We Americans put much more stock in the future than in the past, and we value the unknown (or still-to-be-learned) over the known. Upside is speculation, and we are mightily charmed by speculation. The history of our country, from settlement to westward expansion, is one giant land speculation deal. Migrating from the safe known to the risky unknown. The American Revolution had upside. Manifest Destiny, for all its violent Eurocentric jingoism, had upside.

So the appeal of the young doesn't lie in the smaller number of years they've lived; it lies in the larger number of years they've yet to live. Sixteen-year-olds simply have more future than twenty-five-year-olds, more years for us to wager on, more unsettled potential to populate with our hopes and expectations. Privileging the young allows us to live vicariously through those whose futures are longer than ours. We co-opt the years we won't be alive to see—not because we want to live forever but because living here and now is too painful unless we believe there's a future we can shape and envision. Consider heaven: another sort of speculation deal, property development of the clouds.

Looking back now, it's clear to me that Watershed had potential, but Silverchair had upside. Epic bet on the kids and won. The Aussies' major-label debut sold over 2.5 million records worldwide. The twenty-five-year-olds from Columbus sold south of 10,000. When I listen now to the album we recorded back then, I hear in each song a good, but not fully formed, idea. We hadn't done enough living, so we didn't have much to say. Silverchair didn't have a lot to say either, but they didn't need to say anything. Their upside spoke for them.

Ten years after being dropped from the label, I applied for that spot in Ohio State's MFA Program. I knew I was a risky bet. Raw and unproven. Sealing the envelope with a draft of a first fledgling essay inside, I crossed my fingers that the admissions committee would judge me—an aspiring writer who'd barely begun to write—in terms of *my* upside. If they weren't exactly sold on the little writing I'd done, I hoped they'd be enamored with the writing I would one day do.

OSU hedged at first, sliding me onto the waitlist, but I eventually got in, the last one through the door. Three years later, I graduated with my MFA. At forty-two, I published my first book, *Hitless Wonder*, a memoir of the twenty-plus years I've played in Watershed. If there's a downside to being a debut author in my forties, it's that I have a shorter writing future than I would have if I were younger. But I'm betting I have a much deeper well of experience to draw from.

—2013

Writing in the Major Key

One day nine years ago, I bellied up to the urinal next to a fantasy writer named Charlie. This was during the second year of my graduate program in creative writing, and the fiction class that Charlie and I were enrolled in had just finished workshopping a story of mine. After we zipped and flushed, Charlie said, "Hey, man. I heard one of your songs on the radio the other day. Good stuff. Really poppy."

He was talking about Watershed, the band whose budding success had driven me to drop out of college as an undergrad and, years later, whose frustrations had pushed me back to school to try for a master's in creative nonfiction. As Charlie had said, our tunes are poppy—and fast. The kind of songs where boy-meets-and-loses-girl in three chords and three minutes. Every now and then one of them got played on the radio, and I smiled now at how cool it was that a classmate had heard it. "Thanks, man," I said.

Charlie turned toward the sinks. "But here's what I'm wondering," he said. "Why doesn't your prose have that same kind of, I don't know, *concision*, I guess. That same quick, hard burst of *joy*?"

His question stumped me for a second. I'd come out of that day's workshop feeling good, thinking the class had liked my piece: 6,000 words chronicling a disintegrating marriage in the Detroit suburbs, via a painfully detailed backstory and narrated from the POV of (stick with me here) the wife's Guatemalan trouble doll. Clever!

Meta! This story had come on the heels of my first effort, an 8,000-word behemoth that was also about a rocky Michigan marriage, with an even more painfully detailed backstory, this time from the POV of a small-town tow-truck driver. Gritty! With social class sensitivity!

My fiction was positively breezy compared to much of the nonfiction I'd been writing, longwinded essays that left no personal crisis unexamined. My fellow nonfictioneers were largely doing the same, and in our workshops we dissected pieces about death, disease, sexual abuse, and—that ever-present staple—white men plagued with chronic dissatisfaction. Now that I think about it, sitting next to some of my classmates' manuscripts on that workshop table, my essays, earnest as they were, were comparatively lighthearted. But measured against the song Charlie had heard on the radio, a lot of my work was, well, what's the opposite of *poppy*? *Sludgy*?

I don't remember exactly how I answered Charlie in that bathroom, but I probably unleashed a screed about how prose writing gave me the space to delve deep into character, motivation, and the ways in which the past comes to bear upon the present. Because this was grad school, I likely used the word *epistemology*. I almost certainly used *privilege* as a verb.

The truth is I didn't know then why I could write concise and joyful songs but had trouble writing concise and joyful prose. I think I know now. As an MFA student, I didn't yet have the experience or training to write poppy. I hadn't earned the confidence. I thought that in order to be taken seriously, I had to take myself über-seriously. I thought that longer + sadder + darker = more important. I thought that real writers wrote in the minor key.

***

I see now that this was the same mistake I'd made as a high schooler in the mid-eighties, when I first picked up a hand-me-down acoustic. I figured myself to be a smart kid. I was good at calculus and physics, and I dominated American civics. I knew I could easily become a chemical engineer or a lawyer. But those jobs were for pudgy suckers with Sansabelts and comb-overs. I was going to be a rock star. Not some head-banging buffoon but a serious musician, like the guys in my favorite band back then, Rush. But every time I strung together the three chords I knew—A, D, and E—it always came out sounding silly and simple. How could that be? I read Ayn Rand. I was sincere, dammit. Striving to be intense. I wanted to write songs that *mattered*. (The italics here indicate that I am bringing two clenched fists to my forehead in tormented earnestness—to be followed immediately by earnest torment.)

One day I brought my acoustic over to my friend Colin's house. He also played guitar, and he had decided that the two of us should start a band, the band that would eventually become Watershed. While I was strumming away on my trusty A-major chord, Colin told me to shift my index finger so that it sat on the first fret of the B-string. I wrestled my fingers into position, and there it was: A-minor, the sincere sound of my sincere heart. Ayn Rand played on six strings. From there I learned D-minor and E-minor, and before long I was writing lyrics like *He finds disillusion here, disillusion there / He drinks from the well of his own despair.* My minorness was boundless.

This reliance on minor keys didn't last long—only all through high school and my first three years of college. But after my bandmates and I dropped out of school and into a rusty van, we learned what disillusion really looked like (playing humorless, five-minute ballads for the bartender and the doorman on a Tuesday night in Charleston, WV), and my sense of what counted as an important song changed. I stopped listening to Rush and started listening to the Replacements. I slid my index finger back to the major position and got to work writing three-minute power-pop tunes.

Why the switch in sensibility? If you would have asked me then, I would have said that I had finally figured out the kind of song I was actually good at writing: quick and catchy. I would have said that I'd gotten better at my craft and that "lightweight" pop songs are much harder to write than "serious" minor key dirges. I would have said that songwriters too often use the minor key as a shortcut to—or a substitute for—meaning, as if minor chords automatically give a song gravitas. I would have said, "Rock songs don't need gravitas. They just need to fucking rock." I would have used those exact words, and I would have been exactly right.

I'm twice as old now as I was then, so I can see that there's an additional element I didn't quite understand. Before I dropped out of school, everything I knew about heartbreak and hardship was purely theoretical. My life was simple. It kicked ass. I was a civics-dominating, Rush-loving, suburban kid with nothing more dire to worry about than talking my mom into letting me see the R-rated *Porky's II* at the megaplex. Because my day-to-day was so poppy, so major-keyed, I had the luxury of tormented earnestness. But as soon as I dropped out of school, hit the road, and started getting my ass kicked a little bit, then I lost the need to write glum and dark songs. When my life edged toward minor, it freed me up to write major. And by then I was a practiced enough songwriter to know how to do it.

***

Sorry for that painfully detailed backstory, but I'm exploring the ways in which the past comes to bear upon the present. And right now, in the present, my life still kicks ass, but it's much more complicated than it was nine years ago when I had that exchange with Charlie or twenty years ago when the band was playing for the bartender and the doorman in West Virginia. Now Kate and I have a four-year-old son and a two-year-old daughter. Now I have to think about the quality of the kindergarten I'll soon be sending my son to. Now I have to monitor childhood speech development and cognitive milestones, and I have to find a way to explain to my kids that yes, we do in fact live on a big blue marble that circles the sun. And yes, some day the sun will go dark.

Now that my life is so wonderfully complex—and now that I'm a more experienced and confident prose writer—I'm trying to write with more sweetness and light. I'm trying to write with self-dep-recation but not self-flagellation. I'm trying to avoid writing (and reading) essays that strike the same minor key notes my own work has struck time and time again: excessive gimmickry, admitting one's own faults and limitations in a naked attempt to gain the reader's sympathy, the inclusion of backstory under the guise of exploring the ways in which the past comes to bear upon the pres-ent but really doing it mostly for nostalgia's sake, exaggerating the innocence of childhood in order to amp up sentimentality.

I'm trying, but it's not easy.

Writing in the minor key is easy—for lots of reasons. From a craft perspective, stories need trouble, and trouble ain't cheery. From a practical perspective, the literary community is one that rewards the sincere and solemn, as most journals lean to that side of the scale. Then again, the fact that last year's AWP Conference—12,000 writers, publishers, and teachers sardined into Seattle's Washington State Convention Center—featured two separate panels on how to inject humor into creative nonfiction suggests that writers already suspect we've been taking ourselves too seriously.

Mostly, though, the minor key is easy because the material presents itself so easily. Death and suffering are everywhere. So are beauty and happiness, of course, but we often avoid writing about them because we don't want to seem Pollyannaish. Safer to go either sad or ironic. Which, by the way, is how "important," hipster bands typically cover mainstream pop songs: with either a whisper or a wink. Both ways can be cowardly.

***

After starting work on this essay, I put it aside for two weeks so that Kate, the kids, and I could travel to Ohio to spend some time with Kate's mom, who, according to her doctors and home hospice care workers, had only a few days to live. I hate to admit this, but while we were staying at my mother-in-law's house, essentially waiting for her to die, I found myself processing the events not so much as lived experiences but as potential essay topics. Needless to say, all of those topics were dreary. An afternoon of shopping became "Buying My Son His First Funeral Suit." An excellent curried-chicken salad dropped off by a neighbor became "The Last Grape on the Serving Spoon." And, yeah, I know it. Despite my original intentions, this essay, the one you're reading now, took a sharp turn toward the minor key. Like I say, I'm trying, but it's not easy.

Maybe I can learn from my mother-in-law. She was a piano teacher, and the hospital bed in which she spent her last days sat in her living room, two or three steps from the piano bench. A few hours before she died, she smiled and told all of us who were gathered around her bedside that when she looked back on her life, "It was awesome."

In the moment that was as minor as minor gets, she played one last resounding major chord. A quick, hard burst of joy.

—*2013*

This Machine No Longer Kills Fascists (Did It Ever?)

This isn't the essay I wanted to write.

When I first sat down to draft a piece about how music influences our political dialogue, I figured I'd happily confirm what we already know. Of *course* music shapes politics. It's practically a Newtonian law. *Objects at rest, stay at rest; For every action there's an equal and opposite reaction*; and *Music gives voice to social movements, inching us ever closer to our best and most enlightened selves.* Forever and ever, amen.

Because we take the premise as a given, the argument would make itself. I'd just point to Bruce Springsteen and Steve Earle, Bob Dylan and Phil Ochs. I'd dig into the catalogs of Ani DiFranco and Joan Baez, Marvin Gaye and Bob Marley and Public Enemy. I'd cite lyrics that precipitated political movements, quote songs that bent humanity toward peace, justice, and equality. Or maybe I'd just cut-and-paste the words to Woody Guthrie's "This Land Is Your Land" and be done with it. Case motherfucking closed.

But the more I think about the mingling of music, politics, and social progress, the less I'm convinced of music's relevance. The very idea of a folk singer or a protest song seems quaint and outdated, like a fireside chat or a whistle-stop tour.

I want to believe music makes a difference. I really do. But I'm not so sure.

***

The notion of music-as-political-force has been perpetuated largely by the music *industry*—self-congratulatory and sanctimonious from Woodstock on down. But if musicians can effect social change, wouldn't right now, with two wars and congressional ineptitude and the country mired in the Great Recession, be a good time to start?

***

It could be that "effecting social change" is asking too much of the art form. Because music (*popular* music, anyway, which is the only kind with a big enough audience to matter) only offers two clear policy directives: 1. Party! and 2. Buy shit!

***

As soon as the news broke that Osama Bin Laden had been killed, Miley Cyrus's "Party in the U.S.A." became the national fight song.

As I type this, "Last Friday Night" by Katy Perry sits at the top of the *Billboard* Hot 100, a song that implores us—per the above directives—to dance on tabletops, take too many shots, and max our credit cards. And then do it all again.

Number two on the charts? "Party Rock Anthem" by LMFAO.

***

Recession? What recession? No, no. Nothing to see here. That's no iceberg. The ship's not sinking. Just keep dancing. Keep dancing, goddammit.

***

In middle school, I believed in the power of music with an apostle-like fervency. The way I saw it, all those men in high places could help us change our reality if only they'd scribble Rush's "Closer to the Heart" lyrics onto their legal pads during Senate committee hearings, as I was doing during civics class. In the unlikely event that a Canadian power trio held no sway with our elected officials, then Judas Priest had already plotted the anti-establishment back-up plan: Breaking the law!

But now I'm frighteningly close to middle age, and I don't need a civics textbook to tell me that musicians don't set the political agenda. Think tanks, policy wonks, and lobbyists do. They frame the issues and supply the ready-made arguments. They don't just give us the ideas; they give us the language to express the ideas. We're spoon-fed a whole new vocabulary: *Obamacare* and *liberal elite* and the talking point that says any assertion that rich folks should pay more in taxes is tantamount to *class warfare*.

***

The music industry gives us Ke$ha and "TiK ToK."

***

When I was a kid, FM radio and MTV taught me what to worry about and what to think. Now it's NPR, MSNBC, and Jon Stewart. This is why I know ten times more about the federal debt ceiling than I do about my own mortgage.

***

Confession #1: I totally love Katy Perry's "Last Friday Night."
It's a near-perfect pop song, catchy as hell and masterfully arranged—even the cheeseball sax solo from Tower of Power's Lenny Pickett. It does exactly what it's supposed to do, which is to say it makes me want to shotgun six beers, choke down a handful of trucker speed, and forget about the crumbling economy and the wars in Iraq and Afghanistan for a night. Or for three minutes and

fifty seconds, which, given that I've got a two-year-old at home, is all I can really commit to. Babysitters ain't cheap, man.

***

Even if today's radio hits are almost entirely about escapism (Party!) and commerce (Buy shit!), part of me—the part that still yearns to believe—feels compelled to argue that this wasn't always the case. What about the '60s? Back then, when the times they were a-changing, didn't music help to bring about that change?

Maybe a little, I guess. But for all the baby boomer, flower-power protest bullshit, did any of it stick? Today the boomers *are* the power. They're running the institutions. Doing the banking and warring. The Woodstock Generation got us into this mess.

Meet the new boss.

***

So let's go back even further, to Woody Guthrie, anti-capitalist champion of labor unions and migrant workers, who famously stuck to his guitar a sticker that read *This Machine Kills Fascists*.

In 1944 he recorded "This Land Is Your Land," an angry response to Irving Berlin's sentimental rubbish, "God Bless America." In the fifth verse, Guthrie stops singing about sparkling sands and diamond deserts and gets down to socioeconomic business. He mentions seeing people—*his* people—standing hungry by the relief office, and he wonders: *Is* this land made for you and me?

The year Guthrie recorded that song, the richest one percent of Americans controlled twelve percent of the pretax income. By 2008 the share of the richest one percent had almost doubled—to twenty-one percent. Today the income gap between the richest and poorest Americans exceeds the gap during the Great Depression. Even with unemployment and home foreclosures soaring, stores like Neiman Marcus and Nordstrom are selling out of seven-hundred-dollar

Louboutin pumps. Profits are up at Louis Vuitton, Gucci, Givenchy, and Yves Saint-Laurent. BMW, Porsche, and Mercedes-Benz all report surging sales.

The fascists ain't dead. They won in a landslide.

***

Everybody knows this. The question is why aren't we more pissed off about it? Why aren't we smashing storefronts? Chucking bricks? Breaking the law? Why aren't we, like those rioting Brits earlier this summer, redistributing the wealth one stolen iPad at a time?

***

Confession #2: I am a musician.

I've played bass, sung, and written songs for twenty-five years. And what momentous political message has my band sent? I'll respectfully submit the chorus to "Black Concert T-Shirt," a song I wrote:

> *We wear all the latest clothes*
> *We see all the coolest shows*
> *Bouncers at the nightclubs let us in*
> *Wouldn't take one day back to live it again*

Party! Buy shit!

***

Right now at cafepress.com you can buy a *This Machine Kills Fascists* coffee mug. Fifteen dollars.

***

On an October evening in 2004, I stood with 10,000 other like-minded liberals on the Ohio State campus, watching my hero, Bruce Springsteen, play an acoustic set in support of the John Kerry campaign. We squeezed together on the grass of the South Oval, craning our necks for a glimpse of the stage, where The Boss was belting out "The Promised Land" and "No Surrender," backed by a huge banner that read *A Fresh Start for America.*

I was born in the Vietnam era, a child of Joan Baez–loving peace-niks who took me to war protests and George McGovern rallies. But that was their war, their candidate, their music. This—Iraq, Kerry, Springsteen—was mine. I felt grown up, empowered. As Bruce brought Kerry onto the stage, the audience let out a roar that seemed to rise up in waves, and for a moment I believed this *was* a fresh start. Iraq may have been proof that we'd learned nothing from Vietnam (unwinnable war against a nebulous enemy, built on spurious evidence), but from this point forward, at least, we'd get it right. Standing in the crowd, on the college campus, staring up at the musician and the politician, I felt a stab of, dare I say it, *hope.*

Which quickly gave way to something like sadness. The crowd's enthusiasm seemed to be fueled more by our proximity to two famous people than by a unified push toward a start, fresh or other-wise. Sure, the event had all the trappings of a meaningful happen-ing: the banners, the signs, the chants, the slogans, the speeches, the cameras, the spotlights. And everything looked perfect, down to the carefully selected group standing behind the podium, as diverse and multicultural as a Benetton ad. But the whole thing struck me as empty and pointless.

In thirty years, there'd be another war, another candidate, another musician. This rally wasn't a political movement; it was political theatre, successful only because it so flawlessly imitated the previous generations' rallies, with Springsteen standing in for Guthrie or Ochs and Kerry playing the part of FDR or McGovern. It was pure simulacrum, meaningful not for what it was but for what it referenced. Our cheers represented a collective nostalgia for a past that most of us had only read about in books or seen on TV.

Look at me! I'm at political rally! I've seen pictures of these things! I've watched the black-and-white footage on the History Channel!

***

A month earlier, in September 2004, Green Day released *American Idiot*, which is both political and a masterpiece. But like the Kerry rally, much of *American Idiot*'s power also lies in what it references, namely The Who's "A Quick One While He's Away" and *Tommy*. And maybe this is my age showing, but rather than being a call to arms, a Green Day concert (high ticket price, huge arena) is mostly an exercise in passivity. We sit in the audience, sipping our eight-dollar beers, not raging ourselves but instead watching Billie Joe Armstrong rage. This too is not politics but political theatre—which makes it no surprise that *American Idiot* ended up on Broadway. Like *Tommy*.

***

The primary aim of pop music is to sell records, so by necessity it is *reactionary* rather than revolutionary.

***

Despite the title, the Beatles' "Revolution #1" is a reactionary song. It worked both sides of the fence. On the one hand, it banked on the revolutionary fervor that pervaded the culture in 1968, but at the same time, it mocked that fervor, especially as practiced by faux-revolutionaries long on talk and short on solutions. We all want a revolution. We all want to change the world. That's what we say, anyway. "Revolution #1" wasn't intended to produce a revolution so much as provide a critique of an ineffectual one.

***

Rather than leading the culture in new (and possibly threatening, which is to say *noncommercial*) directions, music becomes popular (and commercially viable) by encapsulating movements that are currently bubbling up in the culture.

So maybe the best music can do is give clarity to what's already happening. Maybe that's all we need from it.

***

Can Bruce Springsteen (or any other musician) get a real, live political movement started? Shoot, The Boss can barely springboard the career of a band he loves.

For years, Springsteen has tried to spread the word about Marah, an incredibly great but fairly unknown group that originally hailed from Philadelphia. He invited the band to open for him at Giants Stadium. He's been known to show up at their gigs and occasionally jam with them on stage. And still, if you stumble upon Marah at a bar tonight, you won't have to wait in line to order a beer or take a piss. There probably won't be enough people in the crowd to fill the E Street Band's private jet.

And that's the difference between being a musician nicknamed The Boss and being an actual *boss*, CEO-of-a-multinational-corporation-style.

***

In the music business, the power has always resided with the people that control the means of promotion and distribution (the record companies) rather than those that control the means of production (the talent). Even in the age of vinyl albums, lots of bands could get records made, but very few of those bands could get their records heard and, by extension, sold.

But now the Internet has opened the distribution floodgates and flattened the hierarchy. Because bands can easily produce, promote, and distribute their music outside the traditional record company system, they're now theoretically free to write songs whose primary aspirations aren't strictly commercial, songs about politics or social issues or harboring secret fantasies of freaky sex with woolly mammoths. And yet most bands, mine included, are still busy trying to write the same old noncontroversial songs that a huge record conglomeration might snatch up and take to the bank.

The Internet has liberated musicians from the stifling corporate profit model, but what are we doing with that freedom?

**

The sad truth is that most musicians, whatever their politics, don't want the job of leading a political movement. I sure don't. I'm liberal as they come, but I'd just as soon leave the dirty work of spreading the liberal agenda to MoveOn.org or some other 501(c)(4) nonprofit.

**

So is anybody singing about home foreclosures? Is anybody taking up the cause of hunger and poverty? Where's the new Dylan? The new Woody Guthrie? Even if the machine can't kill fascists, isn't it still a shot worth taking?

**

Rage Against The Machine seemed up to the task, at first blush anyway. They wrote songs that rally against racists and warmongers and speak on behalf of the poor and disenfranchised. To wit, a song like "Wake Up," which calls to task the vast judicial and governmental network whose primary function is to keep everybody calm (i.e. not breaking the law) despite the huge chasm between the haves and have-nots. Later in the song comes a call to, à la Cassius Clay, take down the fascists with a bomb-like punch.

But all these populist good intentions are undermined by the fact that Rage was signed to Epic Records, a division of the Sony megacorporation. The band sold their publishing rights to Sony ATV music. Let's face it: Rage Against The Machine *is* The Machine, the rebellion fully co-opted by the corporate superstructure.

When Rage finally decides to take a swing at the fascists, Rage themselves had better duck.

***

As Thomas Frank wrote in 1993, "There are few spectacles corporate America enjoys more than a good counterculture."

***

Like Rage Against The Machine, my band was once signed to Epic Records. Unlike Rage, we were never offered a fat publishing contract. If we had been, we would have reached for the pen so fast one of us might have separated a shoulder.

***

Lots of musical acts seem willing to take political stances; however, as with Rage Against The Machine, there's always a *but*.

Lady Gaga is an activist for issues like gay marriage and immigration reform, but she's much more political offstage than she is in her songs, most of which are appealing precisely because they sound so apolitical.

Das Racist sings against injustice and intolerance, but does anyone really think they're influencing political discourse? If not for my wife's subscription to *New York Magazine*, I'd have thought they were skinheads from Munich rather than brown-skinned dudes straight outta Wesleyan.

Then there's Bono from U2. He does a lot of good work for the world. But jeez, man. With a net worth pegged at $900 million, he's got more in common with Bill Gates and Warren Buffett than he does with any folk singer I know of.

***

Surely there's a new Guthrie or Dylan or Springsteen out there somewhere, writing protest songs, trying to light the requisite fires under the requisite asses. But unless he (or she) gets swallowed up and commodified by the exact same corporate and political superstructure he's rallying against, we'll probably never hear of him.

Let's say he somehow became popular enough to enter the national consciousness. What use would we have for him? Is agitation even what we want from music? Do we want to be reminded that our people are hungry? Do we want to be made uncomfortable?

When the ship is sinking, what would we rather do—engineer the rescue or keep on dancing?

Besides, when it comes down to it, don't we kind of love corporate greed? Wouldn't most of us side with Donald Trump or Richard Branson over some half-a-fag pinko-commie folk singer?

***

What the world needs now is another folk singer, the band Cracker sang, *like I need a hole in my head.*

It's hard for me to believe, but that line is now almost twenty years old. Back in the early '90s, it struck me as self-deprecation, disguised as an iconoclastic butchering of music's sacred cow. Now I'm saying it marks the precise moment when pop music gave the game away, when even the musicians recognized the futility of a musician lighting the path forward. Fifty years after Guthrie's "This Land Is Your Land," we'd finally eaten our own.

Because this machine doesn't kill fascists after all. This machine, it turns out, kills folk singers.

—*2012*

Acknowledgments

Many thanks to the editors of the following publications in which these essays originally appeared, often in slightly different forms:

Barrelhouse—"This Essay Doesn't Rock" (2006) and "Barreling into Uncool" (2008)
Bending Genre—"Writing in the Major Key" (2014)
Bloom—"The Upside Addiction" (2013)
Cimarron Review—"The Low Season" (2007)
Creative Nonfiction—"The Botch Job" (2014)
Fourth Genre—"The Bodyman" (2008)
Ninth Letter—"Tricoter" (2007)
The Normal School—"The Mercy Kill" (2012)
Passages North—"In Any August" (2008)
River Teeth—"Partisans" (2016)
Small Spiral Notebook—"Two Haircuts" (2007)
Superstition Review—"The Get Down" (2016)
Waccamaw—"Simpatico" (2008)
White Space—"This Machine No Longer Kills Fascists (Did It Ever?)" (2012)

Joe Oestreich is the author of three books of creative nonfiction: *Partisans, Lines of Scrimmage* (co-written with Scott Pleasant, 2015), and *Hitless Wonder* (2012). His work has appeared in *Esquire, Creative Nonfiction, River Teeth, Fourth Genre, The Normal School,* and many other magazines and journals. Four of his essays have been cited as notable in the Best American series, and he's received special mention twice in the Pushcart Prize anthology. He teaches creative writing at Coastal Carolina University in Conway, SC, where he directs the MA in Writing program.